THE LONG BOND:
Selected and New Poems

ESSENTIAL POETS SERIES 270

Canada Council **Conseil des Arts**
for the Arts **du Canada**

ONTARIO ARTS COUNCIL
CONSEIL DES ARTS DE L'ONTARIO

an Ontario government agency
un organisme du gouvernement de l'Ont

Canada

Guernica Editions Inc. acknowledges the support of the Canada Council
for the Arts and the Ontario Arts Council. The Ontario Arts Council
is an agency of the Government of Ontario.

We acknowledge the financial support of the Government of Canada.

ALLAN BRIESMASTER

THE LONG BOND:
Selected and New Poems

GUERNICA
EDITIONS

TORONTO – BUFFALO – LANCASTER (U.K.)
2019

Michael Mirolla, General Editor
Elana Wolff, Editor
Cover and interior design: Errol F. Richardson
Cover image, *Curvature* – Monoprint (detail) by Holly Briesmaster
Guernica Editions Inc.
1569 Heritage Way, Oakville (ON), Canada L6M 2Z7
2250 Military Road, Tonawanda, N.Y.14150-6000 U.S.A.
www.guernicaeditions.com

Distributors:
University of Toronto Press Distribution
5201 Dufferin Street, Toronto (ON), Canada M3H 5T8
Gazelle Book Services
White Cross Mills, Lancaster LA1 4XS U.K.

First edition.
Printed in Canada.

Legal Deposit – Third Quarter
Library of Congress Catalog Card Number: 2019930490
Library and Archives Canada Cataloguing in Publication
Title: The long bond : selected and new poems / Allan Briesmaster.
Other titles: Poems. Selections
Names: Briesmaster, Allan, author.
Series: Essential poets ; 270.
Description: First edition. | Series statement: Essential poets series ; 270
Identifiers: Canadiana 20190049944 | ISBN 9781771834667 (softcover)
Classification: LCC PS8553.R459 A6 2019 | DDC C811/.54—dc23

To My Community

Allan Briesmaster's Previous Books

Full-length Books of Poetry

Weighted Light (watershedBooks, 1998)
Unleaving (Hidden Brook Press, 2001)
The Other Seasons (Hidden Brook Press, 2006)
Interstellar (Quattro Books, 2007)
Confluences (Seraphim Editions, 2009)
Against the Flight of Spring (Quattro Books, 2013)
River Neither (Aeolus House, 2015)

Shorter Books

The Tunnel Through the Trees (Micro Prose, 1999)
Phantelles (Aeolus House, 2003)
Urban-Pastoral (LyricalMyrical Press, 2004)
Pomona Summer (Hidden Brook Press, 2004)
Galactic Music (LyricalMyrical Press, 2005)
Temple of Fire (LyricalMyrical Press, 2008)
After Evening Wine (Alfred Gustav Press, 2011)
Twenty-eight Sonnets (LyricalMyrical Press, 2014)
Pod and Berry (Aeolus House, 2017)

Contents

from *Weighted Light*
(1998)

Text-subject

Lying here slightly under you on my pale sheet,
I need you
(for starters) to see
me looking good, off-top,
and toward the toe.
I mean for you then to
begin slow and, please,
not hurry through.
I mean for you to look with more
than a quick eye, too –
than even the mind's eye – and bring
many unpracticed senses in
to play. The whole array.
I want you to peer at more
than my bone skin and hair – in an
overhead mirror as it were …
I want you deeply dreamily to
stare, altogether there;
as well, touch, taste and stretch and flare
your way through me.
And I wish you, oh most feelingly
to see
this moist totality,
and with a not excessively
intense nor too relaxing
climacticity,
burst out and swallow and be swallowed and
merge and disperse with me,
again, again, in sweetest vacancy; –
and even after then
hear calling and recalling,
flowing depth on depth,

the silence glowing
beyond my last lapse: and closing back
like a cloud-lancing healing wound
of an utterly quiet reverb-
erant sound.
                    Which
will have gone on delving, after, evermore profound
into the selfsame fertile silence:
bound,
re-bound,
and base, and under-ground.

Mother and Girl

In a flare of sun on a corner,
young willow-woman with
long summer arms like wands
lifts, lifts
her giggling three-year girl in-
to the wind.

They spin white
skirts that billow, mirroring
each other; a touch
balances the forms, tender
and wild; one swirls
both higher and they are
planet and sun:

whose double smile
flashes beyond
the rim of laughter, back
between eyes locked
whirling
aloft this rootless world.

... Till in changed light, my bus
groans, turns, and
the ring of vision
wobbles, almost lost
among clouds ... jostlings
in the shade and dust.

Reedy River

Such a reptilian repose   you little
brown   wound river!   Safe asleep within
your so broad green   inviolable borders of reeds
More   a fixture in this wilderness
than the massed beaver- and man-bitten trees you keep
at distance   Unhistorical
as those far rounded cliffs you   or
old glaciers maybe   once unmade

A "slowness" is too   fast a word
a "somnolence" too lively for
your   elemental going-in-place   As "glass"
is too rough   for the top of this
cool darkest   darkbrown onion-broth

You are that broth really   your surface
isn't even a skin: its one
clear millimetre   the sole clearness you'll reveal
No more an animal or vegetable   than
you are vein of   cooked silica

Still you have life   Your brimming flow
is muscled   And like any live river you
body the slow simplest Physics   of the Fluid Slither:
a flat sidewise architecture   languid
striving for the one   attainless "S"

Hence all   the nearly looped sinewavey curves you make
though yours especially   are rhythmed ungraphably
into a jungle   regularity

Besides   you're full of motes   (at least
the under-translucence up near your surface is)
dust that's   alive or was: in myriad and sodden species
You are jellied almost   by their ichors

So you spawn   and nourish all
those glistening knob-eyed frogs   each dark
lump that floats deadman   and agoggle and alone
in its own   reedwalled labyrinth

And on a windless day like this   you
lift   the breath-swept iridescences of the
air-stabbing dragonfly

      ***

Now I remember when   seven
my grandfather teased me   that the loud "darning needles"
would sew up my ears
Later I read   what voracious mouths their
long nymphs are   down in the depths

Which holds a moral possibly   about
surface   being the one   only trysting-place
for an eyed loveliness
                And while
a warm heart   always will listen after
the internal echoes   not for hollowness
it's true: to dive   or slice into
the dark and liquid pouches of the world   can
tangle us   where all things drown

      ***

The grandfather once also   after we'd been fishing
in the same slow river of the dragonflies
spoke of it being   an "Old Man"   like "Time"

But even if that thought   or any
was new to a boy   and
the sententiousness and drift alike escaped him

its expression   having taken voice
out of a place that man well loved   (whose
surfaces he loved)   although
in broken accent   stood alive and true

       ***

A river   any river too is   I can now see clearly
alimentary   yes   cloacal
But if it's lying smooth enough before us
the wide Surface turns   to much the deepest part
so far as it contains the skies

And you   little brown river   hold
on your thin surface this clear moment
certain treasures greater than the skies

You hold a thousand waterlilies   those
celestial palenesses with scent of anise
rooted in your lower ooze and flow
And you uphold   in my canoe
a living woman and a living girl
who look off now   past the grey distant cliffs
and up   reflectively
at the blue empty surface and breadth

of dry heaven

Golden Delicious

Bagged from fluorescent stores, they're mealy. Jello-flavour.
Greens and most reds keep in a juicier crunch. But go
out on a farm the tail end of October, pick some live, and then
your taste loads colour and a tone beyond

the label. – Though I can't say which feels better, savouring
your choice among the yellow rows, or the sheer seeing ...
after-imaging small planets that droop such rich light from tips
to bases of the laden trees. But best is when

the child beside you reaches and tastes – to be
there with her at the core of autumn while across
time, you recall. ... Holding the cool of the fine sallow skin,
pale, freckled, evenly covered in the palm

with tiny scars, that turns golden again, a branch-
length off, or higher, when the sun steps through cold cloud
onto her ladder, and touches the boughs around
her arm. Golden-haired girl, there where the steady fruits

bloom and have boomed weighted light above
the pungent crush and bruise toward cider. Where
earthly coronas unwrap in the eyes that now
reopen childhood-deep, and tongue becomes

less cloudy. So then the crisp tart nectar fountains
in the mouth, unsealing vaults of health that stay
awhile, before the lapses, mostly blind, in wax
and brazen hunger toward shopworn fools' gold.

In Curved Light

Cold sparks. No vertical heaven any more
than an indefinite void. Light bends, respiring
the burst ovum, the prime flame. And we swallow
this vision. On synthetic faith. In, straight.
Capsule of global science: minds ajar.

You feel a plausibility hung through
the silence under the still trees newly bare.
Except the star-commingled branches tremoring.
They're not asleep yet; it is the outbreak-time
of the November buds. Light weight, on emptiness

of the invisible keystone in earth's arch:
with distant city a sigh, smudgy glare almost
forgotten by this idyll. Soon we'll turn
back to the cottage and build fire. Enough
away, no end-user can page demands.

Data and ergs. That's all? The wild of stars
dwindled as earth's membrane shrank, and lost
the redolence. Be by me then: your own
scent healful in its round, lightless rays.
At least until the fuming roar at dawn.

Waking

after Octavio Paz, "Before the Beginning"

A pale shadow rustles.
Fragmentary intonation
of pre-dawn. Our small room here
in wherever, the little bed, retain
two almost coupled bodies, though in much
of my thought I am sailing far
alone.
          Time's horizontal whetstone starts
to grind the earliest minute's edge.
You inhale, exhale still in uncut flow
along another river. Stranded both
by flesh and by this doubling dream.

You pulse. I quicken: and subside. But sense,
behind your sealed eyes, a grown sprout
of light. With any structured land
persisting drowned, slow seconds waver and slip on
amphibious banks. Tall shoal. What do
I know, beside the dark-red radiation
from our blood?
                    Your rise and fall are tidings,
dim pushes of sargasso at
the amazonian mouth. ... I
listen: you, or they, again incant
the immemorial phonemes that began
the sentence of this world.

The Sprig

after Pablo Neruda, "The Skin of a Birch"

Like a sprig of mint we rub,
you are a velvety and keen
aroma.
Referencing your eyes, in any month,
I conjure
summergreen.

Although I'll never name
your original name,
without it there could be
no language.
                    Poems are
inscribed with lips –
and I beg them now to seal awhile
so I can wholly hear the song
of your fragrant sun.

I'm groping for some words to hint
how my spirit hesitates
on a thin isthmus between oceans
like a pennant in a limp gust.
And not seeing, not feeling who
you are,
I would die here,
though my end might be attributed
to a collapsed metabolism
or black tangle of neurons
in a shamed fuse-box brain.
I admit, time leaks.
It whistles to me like the widower-bird
from a slashed forest.

Even while my sight still lay
gauzed in mist antecedent to
your dawn,
I already had two pairs of eyes – yours, mine.
Don't ask how this has changed since,
for it is time alone that changes,
old roué always refurbishing his wardrobe,
while I'm off hiking the bare lean hills.

Through one late spring, before you,
every kiss clothed me with light
in the bed
of one or another of the distance women
(whose given names might be
Laurel, or Iris, or June),
and it became a salutary habit
to stride between tentative beds outfitted
in a new near-love.

But before those, you
are.
So you remain:
the First One, earliest beginner, stirred
into her steady quickness
from sparkling dust, from the moist blent breaths
of ocean and of heaven.
Initial dove.
Radiant one, at heart
of every circle spread
from every wishing coin
dropped now and dropped again
in every greengold pond.
Enlightened warden
of my sprawling sluggish inclinations,
keeper of a house of light,

to whose warm altitude
I'll never rise (hard though
you spur me to aspire),
not in this life, only
maybe the next one, the next or next.

Because a sprig of such mint
holds all
the persistent taste of summer,
and stems, unbending
around the titled aromatic earth –
velvet and keen,
into full Spring.

Antipodean

I'll probably never make Antarctica now.
Lessened resistance to cold dims the glamour
icy space once cast, and central downtown habits
yap and pant, louder, their paralyzing mantra,
while Roaring Forties widen the South Sea.
Local winter, slushed, gritted, scraped off, can seem
an abject beast, and I've missed the slash of claws,
the full fang. But a large furry music swooshes, even here,
with the odd yowl. Then in dawn after the freak storm,
there's a faerie drape over edifices, of such tasteful
white. And the snow shadows tinge, cool lavender, and one
sniffs the implausible cleanse in the air.

While a boy I played Amundsen and Peary every January,
across a plain blanched garden and adjacent fields of flight.
Unnamed ranges loomed – mere crests there. Immense glaciers
formed ramps for nervy giant steps much cut, at random
by abysses of an indigo that could gulf battleships.
I outfaced katabatic winds, until the expedition breasted
the high blank plateau where nothing else alive had been.
Plodding, by precise plan, through a zone as vague as vast,
I'd verge on the open core of – what? – near lost within
the unlost world until the mother's voice called dinner …

Only the faintest radiance leaks from there. It can't
be condensed back into sound for my mouth.
But I've since read of Shackleton's resolve,
his knowing when to turn from the transpolar grail
so not one of his men would starve like Scott. – And, too,
there's lastingness in *Mawson's Will*. To admire these accounts
with care – dream them with care – is well. So, for

me, expeditionless inside a flat, fissured
and sighing city loved only for persons here,
a different magnetism drifts, draws my one needle
from Antipodes: toward the midmost landmass's
increasingly accessible own Pole of null;
which I find my self hauling near on rough sledge, bearing
a stripped kit, packed with a few gaunt probes
and the cupped loop of fire fluttering at the wick.

The Luminous Man

I have this other self who stays
in hiding, quiet
under the fabric of my skin almost
not breathing.
When he slips out, he sheds
me like a mis-fit uniform:
to stride the broad, the near, surrounding
shores of the bloodwarm gulf.

His acts
embody, gently,
odd qualities I had thought lost.
– A fervour
unashamed in its own sinew.
Placid strength. A surety.
Intensest ease.

All because you, his consort,
answer,
and you call,
in kind. Lantern
of this flesh. Beckoner
to fallow fields of touch.
To simplest orchard, branching tree
where retuned pulses tremor
along the trunk's ascension
from the caress
by leafy fingertip. Secreted
flame. Liquid
enclosure. Smooth vined arms
and an irriguous
rich-earthen grip.

Toward aching sweet
convulsion of release.

And thereafter, the sea
has withdrawn into heights beyond
horizon, poured and steamed away:
to imbue sky, but also
shrunken, far
inside the cavernous and grotto-like
primeval garden,
back to the limpid spring
cleft through the mantle-rock
with pooled flow deep and sure as any
canopy of marine air.

… Before
such fluid dissipates like sunset,
and selves of light remove
into auroral curtainfolds,
and reliquary lives
find we're congealed
into our surfaces once
more

Tech vs. Earth

Imagine a white hand gripped
around the stony sphere our world:
the rotund arc of which
buckles, the grip's
that big and hard.
                    Blood
or a red sap drips from it,
from both, splashes off lost into space.
From both. For the wounding hand too, partly
ruptures and is scored, parts
get ripped
obstinately by the living and dead surface pieces,
by the breakage and protrusions. (Hear
the leaky hiss? that bass
grumble-and-groan, high whine?)
But eaten also through earth's own
more steady appetite, mouth
of the moth, deep joint-fatigue, a stealthy
freckling of rust …

Yet the mechanic hand just
regenerates, and flexes
in, stiffens: grows
perpetually, as though the brain, if
it had had one ever, long
forgot the way their wrist, for all its
girth, still roots
live nerve, veins, in the shrunken
violated tomb of earth.

Religious Musing

If "the Divine,"
or "the Deity,"
is like the ultimate Elephant, and we
the blindmen of the fable,
o my traditionalist friend,
you seem

to have palmed on your palms the immense
hindquarters and found their
pillared stature fully
satisfactory. Perhaps also
aroma? … Then, here's hoping the
whole bottom never squats on thee!

I, meanwhile, seem to scrape a finger
at fitful intervals along
the flappy leathern spinnaker
of ear. So, catch a shifting and
entirely different wind
thereon, therein.

Heaven help them, though, who clutch
for purchase on the bland sidewall,
any who haul
at scrawny rope of tail,
or, whom the long-swung roguish tusks
impale

Joe Henderson Quartet

From the dark solar
mouth, a torrent of cries
breaks: in rainbows.

Soft freight   slams the night.
– Wheel-clash. – Pistons
carom   thunder over skin.

Plucked throbs   arc across
the bridge of the blood, outwalk
all bars.

One hand grabs the ground;
another hammers embers
into stars.

Fire Music

on a performance by Charles Gayle

In
     the time before time, be-
           fore any
       form of form could claw or
         clasp itself
                 through more
       than a swirled figment of an instant,
only
         energy, without
       bound flamed and
        ran.

             If *that* had
           or could have torn
         a mouth of sound, it would
       make, it would be
SUCH
          wailing

Before
       a truth, a law, ever
            broke from flow,
        parted,
              got set, there soared, there
     poured,
       utter
         freedom:
              the gale
                 roared like *this*: a firestorm's

furor and plasmal maelstrom whirled,
          self-
                    hurled, flew, blew on
          streaming, howling, screaming,
                    like
               what rears, veers even here
          in this dive, thudding pit, thrashed neo
     night club, like what
               sheers, clears in
return-flame,
                         sears
          through our abashed skulls' ears

And down
          the general jail of now,
     erectile, walled with undershade that made
               the day dullgrey, the dark more grey, that smears
          across the chain
                    of ashen days, weak flares
     in dead drums gone out under
                    the El, cool
     bleak steam leaked at pre-dawn on
the grating streets of East, their
          flash & trash, blown by; the exhausts' blears
     off
          the piled, stacked,   forgot-sky-
               violating city –

               Mouth, breath
                    to
               otherwhere,
          go shriek,   screech,   go bone-bare

and snarl, gnash, bellow, tear, and
over-whistle
this all
OUT
for us.
– For
the back-core of us, in this
mis-prison,
within our
stunned-still, our ventless
rage, the bounds unsounded,
the cuffs of ice, out-
rage us (past the
gutter-roll and hit wall) with

your torch of blowing; bore
a
way toward that core, that store-
fury, roared
anterior
to fastenings – that forge before
barred banded melody or any
shore of measure, any-scale
can be –

that
astral heat, star-roil, devoid
of line, of lapse, of
separation, … join

Counter-confuse that
fuse, prior
to falling natal chasm from
cold father earth to mother sun,

play, be
        the spasmal
                coupling of the one
                terror-and-ecstasy:

behind
        which, prior, if
    we wildly find it,
            again soars
(at once revealment and all mystery)

            the fire
                and the fire of the fire,
                freefire,
                        free

from *Unleaving*
(2001)

Leaf for Claire

At a speed unknown to me
your three-year-old strides pass
these cemetery elms – arced boughs
quick-shiny with the silvergold

October. Knowing you cannot grasp
the sombre passion fringing
on gentian sky, nor feel
the least cut of its irony

of light, I only
show you how to chase the
leaves, the flittered leaves *(Yes, catch
that one!)* – your rush

of easy gaiety outleaping
the glitter in the wind; though it
too shifts pace and strides by ...
You won't remember

anything of this, but
now your hand, returned
cool, warm on mine, implants
a vow. – To honour that fierce trust:

and defy
desperate ignorance of any
wax to coat intact
even one turned, fallen leaf

under the breath of time.

In Farther Transit

Let me clear my head: look out the northbound window
the last morning this year that I catch a segment
of the commuted dawnlight riding to work.

So much November green kept unaccountably
on bough and bush atop the cemetery ... greenhoused ...?

Still let it green these fainter eyes, though far
from the wet tint luminous there in May.
And was it I
                    who saw? Or, does this mainly mark –
from off the southering of such hollow sun –
my own disjuncture? dry, unripe decay?

Forward Movement

after Rainer Maria Rilke, "Fortschritt"

The deep portions of my life are pouring onward,
as though a river's margins were widening out.
Things bear enhanced resemblances to me now.
I peer more intimately into paintings,
and feel in closer touch with what is nameless.
As with the birds, my senses raise their wings
out of the oaktree onto the currents of heaven.
And in the lagoons, breaking free of daylight,
my heart moves deeper, as if borne by fishes.

From the Depths

after Georg Trakl, "De Profundis"

Rain falls black on a stubble field.
An oak stands lone and brown.
Hissing wind coils by an empty shack.
Sorrowful evening.

Beyond the village,
the tender orphan gathers the thin corn.
Round golden, her eyes graze twilight.
Her womb awaits the celestial bridegroom.

Going homeward, hunters
found the sweet body
decayed in the bushes.

A shadow, I pass remote
from the dark towns. I drank
the silence of God
at a backwood spring.

Icy metal stalks my brow,
spiders reach after my heart.
A light fails within my mouth.

I found myself past midnight on a plain
strewn with garbage and dust of stars.
And in the hazel glade again,
crystal angels ring.

Skin of Our Vision

These hands travelling
our bodies in the dark
sculpt us new spaces.

There we flood, warm from
such meeting distance, what
smooth viewless light:

to which ... this flesh
is only curtain, while
our breaths unite

over the gulfstream
of twined fiery blood.

Venusian

after Octavio Paz, "Vaiven" ("Sway")

<1>

So we renew
the nocturne, string
the moments out of primordial play,
bud skin, the tongue, the lips and fingers:
open the bloom of space

<2>

Rooted apart from the hurricane
with alternate curved pulse, delving breath
you shed your slip
                                        in a silk pool, showing
the source-place beyond hiddenness:
and jettisoning the mainland cables,
waving mentation by at a slow coast
we launch again on sheeted waters
where, blind to the wreck of day,
the catamaran homes for aeonian isles

<3>

You draw me now as full moon draws a tide;
your gleam itself the gravitation.
A wind footed with cool sparks traces the currents
that pull the iron and salt up my veins:

while deep in night the flotilla of downtown towers
drifts with the planet through unpastured void
whose dust and whirling plasmal energies
rave, until azured out by the sea of our sun

<4>

At prairie's end the high grass dips to a coulee,
    above it an updraft caps in a keening hawk,
the crests on the far side undulate onto foothills,
    a lonely campfire flickers the northern dusk,
full boreal curtains fan from the starry darkness
    that sums my manhood's apex of flung seed

<5>

Scribing transcarnal song

I affirm
the lighthouse torch rotated at sunset
I deny
such a rhythmical measure truly could lie
I exclaim
the gold bough-break from the spiral of time

<6>

(Is it

        ever

                not

                    now?)

Your voice / a chamber of fountains vibrates
I can't hold it all / spelling, binding me green
Your quiet's eloquent too / nest, for heated thought
I've lost my compass / arterial reds redirect
Smile into me / a broad stream bears off the ice
Fusing our longitudes / at once dawn and twilight breach

The valves of day contract, release
and along immovable suspension
cordial fire flares
Now\ever (ribbon of iris
pushes the thunderhead)
these are one
being: fresh morn-star and the eve-

Nerudaland

The body of work of one as huge as Neruda builds, in time – with moving plates of book upon voluminous book – an island continent. Rough spinal crags, veil falls and venous rivers, the swept plains of sand and grass and lined, rectangular crop; the brooding cities that are, at once, blotchy horrendous flowers petalled with unnumberable hurt faces, and concrete-scabbed leaking sores. The great gloom-casting clouds on fronts of a chaotic weather tear: into calm roar and slant of flitting suns; the turquoise meditation of a pond suspends, a brown arroyo races after downpour. Layered, mostly erased ruins. Tilted shacks of thin descendants. The pain of animals, the unpicked fruit, the rinds, a lonely wasted garden, slash and burnoff at a tropic forest, the hell mouthed caldera's belch, above, and glacier's patience; back, to sucking lips and swollen phalluses of oligarchs. Those whom these violate.

Blood disappearing in a gutter. Handgrip on chisel, resolute; on auger, drill. On spade. Deep zones of mineral labour; a tiny side-street shop intent with craft; a goblet, brimming the red wine of speech; an artichoke, a lemon's topaz acid, thistle-spike; and a dew-covered tower, grown from abandoned doors. A woman borne away and away by the rain ...

A plank coffin to shoulder, for the hungry one who weighs the earth. Defiant adolescent. One toddler scrubbed and combed in a poor, immemorial love.

But continent washed hostilely or carelessly by moody sea. At whose rim lean, at last, only infinite night and evergliding, conscious eyes of stars.

You Artists

who have annihilated time with pigment,
your quixotic scattered brush with immortality
is doomed, you know.
The "market value" of your work may soar
after each poor
chaos of a life concludes, but
that work
is moribund, as is
your possible legend.

However delicately tuned
the climate-control in the grand museum,
colours must crack, lines
fade under slow
bombardment of air and light. The gnaw
of oxidation.

If
you artists did not make your art
for that eternity which sleeps
and wakes in the Now,
it would have buzzed, have shouted a few
months or hours and never
held power to re-create us, change over
the creatures we artfully are
since Caves of Lascaux.

Sax

The softclad, slightbuilt tenorman walks onstage wreathed
    in fuzzy peppergrey, an unassuming wizard.
        Gently expressionless out to the mic, except
a small smile. ... He
       plays, and during that whole while none
of him changes. The bodymotion's range stays minimal,
      so every energy will lens
                a quick silver
of thoughts' nuance into serenest fulguration.
    With a quintessent verve. It's the mere shapen sound
      that moves, then, outward, round: from an earned bodily
and spiritous
      heart's-ground. And stemmed, upstalked, from a
lush carpeted, plush canopied earth's and water
     mirrored air's cloud-ground; in re-
          flashed vertical
fire firing a constant variegated stream,
   a calm storm drawn   away but bounding back, on, back.
     ... Constant, the shift among the shaded tone-locales,
insistent the
      insinuous asymmetry
   of pace, on, onto each texural place and in/
    out-scape the notes reach, touch and enter –
        wherever they
conceive and birth. ... Initiate by gesture at
   an olden melody, say "Stella," and we're well
    along. Like spellbound children. A snatch of a song
leans, teeters and
    suddenly blurs into cascaded runs,
   elliptic, tight-fluttered, whitewater wheely, that
    seize, freeze or melt trickling, drip trill,

                          swirlpool, pucker
and bulge, and geyser. Pauses come, bright eloquence
    of pensive silence beating with the rhythm-makers.
           (Knowing the need for rest for resonation.) Leapt
off-angular
        next on a tangent whose logic
    eludes through choppy instants of disintegrance,
        until gracile resolve. Met
                       destination; apt
surprise. Vibrant, from cumular spice. A lambence run
    a gamut. Dis-covering quirks, flexations flipped
        past the limits to the tarnishedgolden axe up-
held rocksteady.
        Effortless wide glide, beyond belief
    of breath. Such is – this heady issuance, elixir,
        this most ambrosial (equally
                   daemonic) aether.

                    >><<

Up there: from sparse beeps, hawk-squeals, half melt us one sole
    caressing plume of a longnote, midrange; veer it, and
        shear through, and deliquesce and spill downbubbling to
a bottomdrop
        to foghorn zone. Arise: reed ghost …
    Each tune, the myriadic voice roves its own free-
        constructive roadpath, never map-
                  directed, yet
inevitable. As the weather. Stakes a theme,
    soon slides the chords ajar, weaving apart from pattern,
        ravels an odd remnant, twists, loops up; archingly
slingshots for home.

… While deep across, the crinkled solos
leaven their in-folds with a coolest fervence and be-
    attitude – but skin-warm, too; ply
                wit edged, wileful
and wild tendril-swaying, wound by the gnarled vine-roots
    to Bean, to Pres, terrible dare of Bird, of Trane
        drawn, built on, housed, and cellar-delved unstoppering
a sure, blent-true
        ownbrew: … you digest it, and it
    does you; all utterly classic but as much, all new.
        Stoking "The 'A' Train" till it turns
                a rocket, then
a submarine. Sonar transformer. Reforging
    old Swing riff, ballad, primal Blue, bop, modal, at
        some hearth of star. Streaking each outroute orbital
on-through to kiss-
        down runway. Or, winged offagain,
    takes us a taper, wisp, a waft, aloftly; or
        draws forth the only curtain that can stanch
                the pour, forming
this ritual: the mouthpiece kept in lips past when
    the bass's turn begins, he tips the spent bell   up
        at heaven, benedictive; lowers back, but holds
that gold column
        a final minute, silently
    and fadingly slowfingering. For why – ? A fast
        clung brotherhood to the next solo;
                loved reluctance
to let this moment go; an envisaged persistent
    overlay of boundless echo; and a friend's affirm
        of quiet faith in neverendings; in such gifted
music's magic
        everlingering.

With Bass

He draws your focus on, strong,
Purely through sound. Though solid
first, with the dusty close-cropped
ascetic. A pinched, pious air.
aloof devotee.

go he's been grooving fierce.
whichwhere the reedcall whirls.
ground. And what hot, freshdelved
what veins deep-pump from there
sax & drums.

keyboard, synth. The ladder of
stretches hero-length, too; no
continual journey. With large loads
he slows, and slews it to a spread
wanding, and

wails, cross-ways. A subterranean
inventiveness miles-past, while
the small cousins, also – quick
Tones that jut, glide, swerve, sting,
lovely ache.

eringly push, relentless though
In ocean-motion, as if of
the tenor's aerial eel,
by way of a wry, scattered sea-
– Until, the Hope-

sooner than some usual plod could.
and burled round, body and face, at
hair, the stubble-beard, he looks
Monkish (without Thelonious). An
But, since

Moving the sound: beneath every
Along alive, rich fluent thunder-
wealths of clefnote, liquid lodes,
before the in-return-listening
Nobody missing

the flow climbs plentiful. The solo
ho-hum, only the surging and the kept-
of rhythmic press left, still, when
throb, or else rows with the bow, tight
eerily scrape/

ascension. – That vents, that scends an
mindful of, the basal "walk." Recalling
guitar, the violin at stratosphere.
fling there and here harshest raw
or, outhov-

with glow. Dark hum of roundglow . . .
a rubythroated whale. Who, like
instinctly skirts cliché-coast, save
flag fly of quotelets, collaged-on.
Cape gained, his mask

evaporates in pitched passion.
agony. An uncontainable
fat 8-shape (where fingers rub,
of eros) and the engaged brain's
prior to launch.

solo's architected apex, you
suffuse hard ions, fuming to
with infrasonic and trans-
the shuddery cloudpoured liftOff.
already

The face-pinch turns: a grimace,
groundMime unites love-making to that
strum, softclaw, creep and jump – warm tons
cold countingdown a padded Shuttle
At least, toward

sense this androgynous woodbeast, doubled,
drop clamp and any brace; now due
spectral roar on flounced flame, for
But, then? But then the earth's
moving too.

And on Drums

Around, behind, through all, our drummer drives
    the counter-lightness. Another younger vet, but his
        cleanshaven jaw is a lean lantern meant for grins.
Cavorting sticks untrap a levitational artillery

of laughter. Plus what? Tricky mix of mischief into
    a whimsy in his bop licks overwraps the serious swinging –
        own, and the collective. The grins have such wattage they
(with many quips in play) coax a smile back

even from dour Bass. Bright chuckling freshet. – Though,
    you look away, it rumbles thunderous enough. And,
        sprightish as may firstglance, fundamental fury
coils. Irreverent toughlivened kit of beaters bent

to puncture any baggy sullen gas. Firecrackling, yes; then
    tremor, heave – grind, pestle the floor into fluid under-
        foot (and -bone), while wobbly cymbals wave-crash, cresseted
in seethe. In hiss … Whisked foam-flicks and big bullet rain

hurrying the hurricane. Snap, lash, and fusillade
    of cachinnation. A slow chop, gapped; rapid whap on bash;
        upcrumple; tossoff conflagration. Yes – all of
this also burns hurt anger, sears the quiet in-between stroke, in

invisible smoke past toothflash, the exultant shout,
    and by wince and by groan goes enwoven, stains the lost
        history, the singed continuum, of such rambunctious jest.
Tears' heavywater saltscalding the inland beaches …

Then still, ultimate buoyancy. His personal joy to set
    and keep the kettle of things at the boil. Roiling.
        'Cause this music won't brood long, can't help but bellyquake
downdankest cells, chortle, and dragonsnort and earth

splittingly laugh as we saunter, safe, near, offsorrow.
   This man-elf of tensile wire lightly owns and sheds this
      visceral vision. He won't hammerthud (is Loki,
never Thor); will clatter jounce ding pummel some, with

ebony weavewave like a fighter feinting 'gainst
   the shade of silence or dull wall of still. Dancingly
      tapping. The rim-nimblest. A strong, sonorous timbre too.
So bonged harmonics inlay tasty solo and the total

bustling romp that's his accomp. Bodying boldly as
   he lances, bobs and bumps – outgoing modesty, a
      sweet cool unabashed by, while (still salamandrine)
thriving in, uptumbling to crisscrash, the furnace grandeur.

Ample wit, to heft two sounded, blowing titans
   with deft limber sinew of its own. Or tickle feather-
      delicate, punchline them to a well rolled, a
whole-shared guffaw.
                      And us who invitedly hear – spur,
                         spire into a happy awe.

from *Interstellar*
(2007)

Only,

      not to stay blocked-off,
not be cut by the trivial wall
from the measure of stars ...

What innerness? except
a lofted sky, the moved heaven
birds plunge through:
                deepened
with the clear, homing gusts.

   after Rilke, "Ach, nicht getrennt sein"

Plea

The west light settles, pink,
on eastern buildings and hills.

Why is it I feel most awake
and strange when the far
objects brighten then draw
nearer-in while they fade?

Don't answer. Before
you abandon me
to impermeable dark, admit
my absence under the moon.

Allowing this life.

Solstice from an Office Tower

Sun after snow, beamed wide under a sky
half trout-scale and a third thin flannel tent
(outside whose blown flaps rifts of azure lie),
unveils a surface largely different

from those I felt I knew – and put in jokes.
This carries beyond gleaming strips of park
and flattop, draws out glints in granite, strokes
whimsy of vanes, of cupolas that mark

centres for muddled power. Icy lanes
turn into radials of shine. Noonday's
whole city throws grand gestures. Bloor Street strains
for the escarpment the hazed sunset-rays

soon couch on; long Yonge leans – it yearns – to flow
past Thunder Bay, embracing North and West,
those fonts of cold. Bluegrey Ontario,
translucid, shows white dints on windy breast

that slide to harbour among brightening quays –
realmed, also, at this huge mood flashing by,
no one knows why. ... Vacant Academies
wait out the holidays, less stodgy, ivy

stripped like pretence; knobbed spires having hinted,
here rests a more tentative *Musée*. Cue-ball
of Planetarium whitens on white. Noise-tinted,
the traffic ribbons its blinks past a swank mall,

while through side-slush, confetti-speck shoppers
bend tuques, flap scarves. Chasmally down, they're flung
identical, on foot, in cars, none shabbier
than others nor less glamorously slung.

Reduced to demographic pigmy-gods,
they model what dead planners guessed our role
would be, below prodigious broad façades.
– Where extremes meet and no object juts dull

or lurks inertly ugly. Never bright,
thick-banded racks of high-rise wanly gleam
like battlements, at least not thwarting light.
All over, lively luminous puffs of steam

tear from the tower-tips as if with wills.
What aspirations and soft under-care
mount below them – to press whatever kills,
emplacing roofs that yield no breath to spare,

that weigh the lifting shoulders, leave them bent
for hefts of hierarchy fuelled by such stress?
Complicit and opposed, how less present
and fleet is one's own shape and own impress,

own conscience of place within place before
a fading star, or an oncoming glow.
Yet now, noon's blaze drives anomie, terror
and dread back at a glance, perhaps. *A crow*,

the only motion higher than my eye's,
save insect-crosses tilted toward their hive –
graceful flake, casting no light – veers and arrives
high on the roof of "The Four Seasons." Jive

regent of carrion. Mutated grafter
on swept-back Nature, sombre sexton, latch
to lonely thought? I swear I hear a laughter,
smirk the nonhuman being lets you catch

sometimes. – Distant and rare as love spent on
this era, moment in it gone from one
who's part, and no part, halfway come unspun.
… Half wild atop this city in this sun.

Pomona Solstice

Whatever swells this risen world's foundation
amid the clarity of the green morning,
but the very sun? The gleam, in micro myriads,
that now tightens the dew. Whole day, before me,
like uncut meadow, and the trees above the path
towering higher through their chiming birds:
oriole whistling, busy for its nest,
the chip and clack of grackle, caw of jay,
and hooded cries of some not caged in names.

I am absorbed, almost, by buoyancy.
How space articulates wish and behest.
Its largesse lifts me from more shadowy grammar,
while the fine light extends far forms. Reclaims.

The leaves twirl speechless phrases, nearly wings.

Fossil Moth

for B. and P.

A scrap of oilblack shale shoved in by the waves
on Georgian Bay shore – look close, and it's embossed
with fossil shells. Their manifold curves and lines
form brown and silvergrey runes, mostly concave:
like imprints of some species of barred-winged moth.

A large lump of such rock, if we're still looking,
could carry side-seams a careful tap will split:
to show clusters in layers, overlapping
chaotic hieroglyphs or logarithms
of transforms pressed on past remotest death.

So, through the cloudless September forenoon, I
and my friend, on our outing-within-outing, picked
at the dark chunks, marvelled a little, and chose
a few to take to the kids at home. – But, through
a moment's access of clear memory, those

two souls at once became not I and not he;
and seemed a studious, inquisitive boy
and his friend prospecting grey shoulders of shale
along a misted Kodiak Island coast
where fossils rose in cliffs from ebony sands ...

Hardly a fleck of feeling blew back, and yet
a vision into that epoch broke straight-clean:
and brought on reverberations of a thought
strong in the belief that somehow they (– that we –)
would learn all there was to know, around our world

of purpose, lineage, inner form, from star
to dinosaur. – Belief: that each would climb on,
to tap at many a hollow vein bearing
the incrustations of primordial lore
like minerals, and find immemorial

underlife strangely immortalized. How well
then (I also recalled), beyond splendour
and surges across that full summer of twelve –
an all-star in our Little League, a patrol
leader in Scouts – I'd liked the new adventures

with that good friend. … Until my parents, moving,
tore me off to the continent's inland side,
where fledgling senses of breath and stretch got limed,
and whoever I thought I was quietly died:
sinking in layers under the common pavement.

)|(

It was the Sunday of that weekend retreat –
at, not by chance, the period of the full moon.
We had songs, baseball, hikes, a sumptuous banquet,
and four Circles of trust, where one could speak free,
while candles quaked and waxes dripped, at our core.

When Bill and I rejoined the conclave of friends,
I thought to pass around one particular find.
And even though my own life-wounds were minor,
I soon felt my sketchier story converge
below stock strata, shelves of stale metaphor …

A change came over the small rock I offered,
after it had been rubbed by the ring of hands.
Perhaps the oil from listening fingertips
bled fresh lustre onto the one barred-winged form,
that let me see: how no one need abandon

the shapes of wings where fossilizers compress; –
not with such flame felt fluttering below-bone.
So I mean now, unburying mine from stone
of shamed, inconsequent years, to re-release
… oh, not some yen for vertiginous knowledge, no

hark-back after quiet maroonings of bliss
forever on the irretrievable shore.
Keeping a talisman that touches heart's thought,
I'll call on friends to alter such lonely lore:
and unseal a far different chrysalis.

)|(

The sun of a dozen years drowned, a life ago,
but the harvest moon still rises. Now I know:
a print of flight embedded in all can well
(with friendly help) soar, sing from the stone – and hold
more than a candle-flare at the fossil stars.

November Trees

near mid-month

How rich, though, stay the few untimely trees
– lean limbs, or thick twigs, gnarled or elegant –
that have kept leaves to themselves, off the slant.
The slight wind, brightly coldly, shimmers these,
and puffs some handfuls into scatters-down.

Indifferent or not, withholders pore
a counter-wane of light through, staining pure
the warm old green, hot yellow, bronze, rust-brown:
swayed, dangled and adorned, refilling now
with under-tone and almost lively glow.

In my season I'll not let such tone go.
On nets of shiny branches, forms more spare
will glisteningly unveil, tomorrow, here, or there:
when every thing bares all it has to bear.

two weeks later

How well-informed the limbs
of the November trees,
replacing the nubbed scars
the leaves left at their tips.
They had no need to know
the thing they were to do.

Subtly the firm-shaped bursts
of new clustering buds,
coloured a fecund rust,
erupt, compact and tough:
act, in the cirque of air,
all that it is they are.

White Passage

The shock of the first snow is
   beauty and strangeness more
      than cold:
as when you are youngest, wind-
   thrown snow – the thicker, the
      more brisk the better – only breathes
exhilaration (hardly sweat
   at all, to take or
      shake it), riding
with no hands, off-grounded,
   body-sailing through the flow,
      the total crest
of youth now brinked
   along alternate childishness,
      to spill onto
fresh foolery and thrill
   and thin-clad daring –
      because this
chill stroke, this foremost open kiss
   pulls out the floor
      of her and your
not-ever-turning-back abyss.

Winter Night, Looking North

after Archibald Lampman, "Winter-Solitude"

Beyond the pallid highrises cutting the sky,
low spinal hills protect strips of dark evergreen,
and up the un-rezoned gaps, the resuming snow's white
gleams on beneath orange-canopied city night.

In this small lane my boot cleats press heavy ice
hardened since rain and thaw; but the thickfallen snow
smoothes the diced grey-jumbled brow on my burgeoning town,
surface and ground, under fresh wide swaths of primal down.

There's enough wind-chill, this hour, to yield solitude,
or give the sense that I breathe free here – apart,
not feeling for others more cold and only alone,
like the long-absent father now entirely gone.

It's so late. Though northern draughts, drawn from cosmic space,
still float a crystal insistence: on truce, on peace ...

Father's Boy

after William Stafford, "Parentage"

My father never belonged to society.
At any time he'd have, at the most, one shy friend;
always remaining strange, dark, and opaque to me.

He held lifelong to a tight pack of opinion,
skirted and scorned many things it could not contain;
beshadowed himself, if stuck beyond that zone.

Now down the midnight well, I'm straining after where
he might have shone the least keenness, pang, or dare.
Blank returns. … A barbed sarcasm, small angers

dart at a clumsy boy slowlearning, learning long:
a muffled edginess, denser skin, polite fear,
in shy societies that let him near-belong.

In the Whitening

after Paul Celan, "Homecoming"

Snowfall keeps on adding its tally
to yesterday's feathers
falling by flying, dream-
walking, bedded, sleep-winged …

White whited layer, upon
obliterate layer. And way-aloft: the
unscalable, indefinite contrail
of the flown-off.

And from below, sore on the sight,
through distance across mound, over crest
rises the weightless
pressure of the unseen.

Every shrunken effigy snatched
into presence displaces a
silenced awareness, like
a coated road-sign.

Only a lone, felt twinge creeps counter:
whipped in the strewn
wind strewing albino
albedo for banner, for wreath.

Vertical Song

But how to climb? Consider the daunt
of the slope – for eye, for tongue.
The pitch-dark rungs. And then
the absolute cold. The sheer,
the tenuous distance.

So you import your
irony to the gap I've
left for it. Applicating
the hang of fatal loss.

The fool I am, I rise and
reach up, again: and the blood
and the bone betray
or deny, side-slipping all down.
Though still I (loftily
as we can) praise heaven ...

Figurative Descent

When teeth of simple limits and the traps of dusk
bear down, you either descend or asphyxiate.

You must relinquish, sink through ground by feel, let go
all that was crystalline, let blur the skins on things
along visceral lava, and conjoin the twisty slide
back within fluid roots incorporating soil.

The squiggle and smudge here lack tips and bases.
No edge, no surface. The sole lampless glow
is the suffused hot infrared of pre-birth.

In it you cave, co-lapse to the spawn-zone
whence existences got expelled. Smear in.

Be with the glob where, inter-touchingly, mind's hands
must muck, brain wholly yield, or such will leave you
sterile. This heart-fundament, looped convolution.
Intone. Ingest its hum: ... till, out again, toward light,
the walls of viscous peristalsis heave you.

Solarities

How simple those ancients were,
who glorified the sun,
thinking it perfect – though its year
did not align evenly with the moon.

At school we learned that this small star
is changeable, has cycles
of relative calm, then times
of sunspot-storms. – Whose flares
disrupt our signals and our powered gear,
and fire the bizarre, waving auroras.

… And that the earth falls tilted on-around it,
and that it also falls
around the centre of the galaxy,
on one of whose spiral arms it tinily shines.

Now in this sleepless morning, wading
the near and narrow solace of the park
in dregs of night and after-film of nightmare –
here, where I see too plainly by my breath
that one more summer's at an end, my eyes
must tear from shredded dream onto
sunyellow treetops –

there, where a brightening goldfinch
turns his plump breast toward *you*, old Sun,
and sings and preens, bathed in warm radiance.

Here, without much nostalgia but a leap
of mental will, selecting memories,
I could applaud the ancients. Try their wings.

Interplanetary

From Earth, no planet feels cold as the stars do.
    You can observe the clear difference even
over the city. A planet won't shiver.

    Saturn and Mars burned fiercely near here, of late.
        Could that "mean" something non-astrological?
    Yes. – Pure phenomena have a gravity

of their own, *pacé* our smudging outgassed spew.
    Thus, to conceive them, past calibration, too,
transports one far from valleys our numbers mar.

    (Pale Saturn's got some really nice rings to it,
        and a Titanic moon, thick with atmosphere.
    But, myths aside, I'd as soon settle on red Mars.)

Apart from myriad downloaded pixels,
    new knowledge liberates – if we clasp, not let daunt.
Science gains room for a charged Spirit to rove.

    "Earth's the right place for love," claims a pastoralist –
        a rather cool chap, from the last age. ... I claim:
We love best when we feel this Earth isn't all.

Interstellar

Yes, not this earth only, for search and stretch of soul.

Which isn't to say I don't love the fecund stars.
Any crisp night well-away from the glowing towns ...

Proliferation: spiked ice; velvet vacancy.
Ordered, almost. Configurable. Dense-and-sparse.
Uncontained emptiness; with spangled plenitude.

A boy in soft bonds you tantalized, olden Stars.
Soon, the conception and math of vast measurements
filtered a high-narrow, recondite expertise,
and the keen yens of those years faded as I fell.

Once, in the era when despair was fashion's faith,
a dour bard termed your sparkling milk "virus of God."
My ground and lift, then, remained Science – fact; fictioned.
I dug "hard SF," not popular fantasies
(even so, holding my time's crush and dread bone-close).

                        *

A star's a lonesome thing, posed far-aloft. And, near,
it beams no radiance: just blasts of torrent rays.
Hydrogen furnace. Raged, spotting, aflare. White Beast.
Corona? Mere plasma. Not quite immortal. Star –
our sun one minor kind, slung on one spiralled rim.

                        *

How easily this lore slips minds that simply look.
Print-informed we may be, but prior instinct rounds,
and overtakes gazes given the chance to clear.
– And? – I *am* lonely, there. Yet, in some way consoled.

Ptolemy and Paz wrote well, to say: *"the stars write."*
They scrawl a broad cosmic scripture (I'd amplify).
How poor we are if blocked from scanning that full page.

Its unpronounceable spell draws me from myself.
Quiets-down, in the depth; stirs, deeply. Up-raises,

ports me ulterior space, and dis-parts from time;
shows selves both lone and re-set, constellation-wise.
(Where inward ponds were torn, a boundless calm came on.)

                              *

Science – I like when you tell us *we are* star-stuff.
Matter's congealed, you say, from stellar death-spasms.
… "Supernovae." Fine! No need, now, to name to me –
or envisage – the soul grown toward a grander star.

from *Confluences*
(2009)

By Ancient Starlight

The stars are shy over the parapet,
and I of them – much as
I aspire to friendship.

But no matter how clear
they ever shine,
my eyes lack scope or scale.

I keep craning, though.
And sometimes your stride

comes closer in, Orion, and
you, Corona Borealis, float
much lovelier, shimmering on
the spherical stream, than shapes
the blank daylight provides.

In thanks I configure for you,
and for some like me, these few
long-scattered and dotted burns
of the black light of words.

Antiquity

Across the distance into the ancient time,
up from the layered tills and the rubble-mounds,
flow traces less than the smoke from extinct hearths
around the stubs of pillars, from staked-out pits
in excavations, through museum cases,
on, among the projects of the living hand.

Labels bestowed on the fragments, notions parsed,
interpolated, spliced, decipher some ways
the avatars, at zenith, plausibly walked
and bonded, kept house, warred, and thought and believed.

Unburnt scrolls, in their devoutly copied fractions,
the bits of shattered tablets, glyphs on half-walls
bewilder with their loose disintegration.
But more than the lopped statues and the defaced
bas-reliefs, the pot-shards, amphoras, and all
the amulets, oil lamps, vials, coins, there are words
whose lips can re-open the long tombs of dust.

Imagination and empiricism,
together listening with their unlike ears,
audit the irretrievable. Fancies, facts,
conjectures, and frail scrapings sift into life
when diligent obsession and adept care
incline the patient pupil to be convinced
they were as ignorant and cruel as we are,
hospitable and charged with naked courage,
fierce, awe-stricken, and noble beyond our reach.

In suffering, in impassiveness toward pain
they dwarf us. And in natural genius:
adjacent to the origins of all things.

* * *

What sages they had when the wide world was fresh!
First law-givers. Before them, the myth-makers.

The rooftops fell. Even the thickest of walls
succumbed to time's and barbarism's rough thrusts.
As offspring of the Vandals and Visigoths,
we linger in the ruins of their ruins,
incompetent to own their virtuous powers,
though sharing flaws that opened the ways to here.

Their scripts fared better, mostly, than did their stone.
Their words continue under-layering ours.
Our twilight still comes tinted with their breath.

Fire Spirit

So we must imagine, and not
      deduce, the dim past.
Let loose the flame that creates,
      unlike what leaves ash.

Bright-hot mental blade – struck across
      the flints of what was.
Ligature for leaping tongues:
      from what was, unto is.

Clairvoyant faith, positing
      an inflammable arc,

the fiercest credence burns on
      through the rinds of the dark.

Archaic Woman

The strict form of the temple won't contain you,
nor the agora wholly shut you out.
The dealers in the words and coins and goods there still
transport you, through the temples of moved thought,
across familial into nameless bounds.

Unthanked, you bore their rising civilization,
nurturing it, without what we call love
from those who looked on passion as dementia,
by the long bond to child, and child of child,
with tight commitment keeping the entire house.

If dowry, quiet tact, fertility,
grace, the whole dark, impassive "feminine,"
were stable, though, what made us what we became?
Only wars and inventions? Invasions, migrations?
You laid your own strong, tender templates down

before The Individual broke into being
from noble and tyrant; while assorted gods,
gross monsters and grandiose heroes muscled the core
of stories and their slight off-centre females
remained curved mirrors for manly desire and dread.

A patience beyond articulate conception,
more deeply absorbed in Demeter than Atalanta,
held fiery ova of hope, and you brooded on them
with tight commitment, taking the entire house
across the familial into the nameless grounds.

If by War

It should be understood that war is the common condition,
that strife is justice, and that all things come to pass
through the compulsion of strife.
            —Heraclitus

But if you mean by "war" *unending struggle,*
hot opposition, rough contention – then
I'm in agreement, ancient sage of flame.

The wedge and ploughshare that impels and drives
the dialectic through our restless lives
wrings constant combat: over scarcities,
for which deep urges and desires make claim
when these can not be portioned or shared out;
and any rule or dictum pits resistance,
arouses and invokes some turnabout.

Every assertion conjures its negation.
We lay waste, clearing paths for newer birth.
Flame's petals yield the seedlings of creation:
hard dragon's teeth sown in volcanic Earth.

Water Sages

(Thales and Anaximander)

And if the source of all is not in myth,
will it be found and grasped somehow by thought?

The gods, no longer operant on things,
become nonsensical to luminous minds
which discern natural laws, make measurements,
are able to forecast the sun's eclipses,
and fix the solstices within their year.

Then, has whatever now exists proceeded
from one material, infused everywhere,
or from some imperceptible principle?

Is the prime universal substance Water,
that feeds and floats this round earth from below;
or is there, behind it, and air and fire,
a limitless constituent, out of whose flow
things separate, and back to which they'll go?

And if that source remains beyond thought's reaches,
in all the discourses and theories since
those two Milesian sages' first exchanges –

might mythic dark still yield a deeper glimpse?

Hestia Exposed

Apollo and Poseidon wanted you
as bride. So, to keep peace within Olympus,
you vowed perpetual virginity
and veiled yourself beside the sacred hearth,
tending – embodying – its life of flame.

Yours is the shy vitality without which
home can afford no safety and no nurture.
Gentle and modest, patient and attentive.
Should some fool ever ask, "What does she *do*,"
the best retort would simply be, "She is."

Está – maintainer of earthen foundations,
grounding the household in the glowing fire
that lets all dwell together without fear,
keeps children snug inside home's inner walls,
cooks favourite food, and lights the ample table.

The old Greeks, with their outdoor public art,
made her few temples and few images,
and fewer tales – though sometimes they invoked her,
placing her central in a pantheon
preponderantly volatile and fickle.

* * *

I think you could be wisest of all, Hestia.
My sole imaginary dread for you
(although this should be plain impossible)
is that you might one day be caught outside
unsheltered, without shawl or woven flame

to wrap you: in a time when homes are shattered,
when primal sense of centre and of floor
lapses until the memory of what "hearth"
and hospitable household meant has flown.
But then wouldn't we cease to have been human?

At that point you might need to marry Ocean
or be the mistress of the imperial Sun,
and take dolphins or eagles as familiars,
if any are left after the reign of men.
Or deities outlast the bond with them.

Autumn came

on time, bearing
the classic, quiet fiery
messages. The clear
code in the ripening trees
and all.

Yesterday I read
on her unprinted gown
of sky (the one
with the goldenrod-and-aster hem)
the welcoming

it would have been inhuman to refuse.
And touched, like Braille,
the embossed volume
she proffered, holding the works
of life and death.

* * *

Back in the full of June, when green-
violet seedheads on the meadow
first embrowned, I had
anticipated, but
language and melody

were missing. Melancholy mixed
with delicious longing gave
plenty to preoccupy
the illiterate heart.
Rainbows would bend

sometimes, after the thunderstorms,
and I adored the way
the cordilleras of the cumulus,
on turning mellowgold,
increased the air,

    then drew apart
    in solemn coral-pink tone
    to a stupendous coast.
    And later, savoured
    the upsprung sundown wind.

* * *

Those days, believing I
loved best the world this one
only shadowed and now and
then tantalizingly
fore-ran,

    I plain ignored
    the singe-off of
    nebulous blossom,
    and left unnoted, after the slate-
    and-ash collapse, above,

how the night city painted
a shroud of steam.
Noon after noon saw dimly my
denial of the lunar
dark. Of solar dark.

* * *

Now in this gifted season,
when mortal music's tremolo
swells field and glade, and the inequity
of night compounds,
the debt

comes legible that I
must pay earth, the maternal sky
and patient friends: without
back-interest of the least
cosmic regret.

Call

Stellar divination,
sheddings of fire and air,
　　You
　　　　vertiginous
lucid rapture
　　fallen from over
　　　　the filling moon,

take me toward words
　　with precise teeth,
enraged, to rend
　　the blank, dull, numb –
　　　　every such drawn
barrier.

　　　　– Until
　　and until
　　　　the long-brokenness
itself　　break, and be
　　broken through.

Riddle

I am a lantern at noon, straining
to cast a midnight shadow that
will flicker a darkness not invisible
past any sunset, past any dawn.

I am a current in a long river
bent to deposit mineral traces
and crystal lattices in future stone.

I am a breath of an air aspiring
to birth snow-flurries onto an empty
desert valley, so new flowers blow.

I am the whirling millionth seed
intended to end as a permanent root –
and lantern-tree whose thick shape of shade
prints the ground above and below.

A Few Kinds of Blues

Fresh blue of distance.
Of the scattered sunlight,
vast, and safely transformed
… over domed air.

Blue surfaces, blue waves
that wrinkle and calm,
and mirror more deeply
the tint within
the clear ocean up-above.

And the earthly
edible blue of the only
blue foods I can think of –
blueberries and plums.
Oh – and blue cheese!

Then the blue of your eyes. That, most.
And pale blue of your veins.

So why, then, should blue stand
for sad?

On Music

after Rilke, "An die Musik"

Music: the breath of statues.
Perhaps, the stillness in paintings.
You, speech where all speech ends.
You, time stood-upright on the heart's path.

Emotion –
and for whom? Metamorphosis
of emotion to *what?* A hearable landscape.
Strange locale, Music. Grown out
of our own heart-spaces. Out of the Inmost,
climbing us, to press beyond.

A sacred departure: when the Within
stands as remote
as the other side of the air.
Clean,
unbounded, and not
anyplace where we live.

Du Fu's Pines

China, 8th Century (after a literal translation)

My four pines, when they were first transplanted,
stood just over half my height – and now,
after three years, they match me. Carefully,
I look them all over. ... The roots hold strong,
the branches somewhat battered, but they
stretch their thin arms in shiny deepgreen.

I've escaped the rebels. I'm home. Spring grass
floods my yard, and my fence around the pines
is broken. Peace has not returned, so
I cannot claim this empty house, where
little is left. Much was ruined. Still,
to be back here is happiness. The caress
of a soft breeze brings a feeling of youth.

My pines – grow tall, and spread your shade.
I, a man without roots or ties, am your friend.
I sing poems. Consequences of these times
will soon drop away. And what use to speak
of my days to come? But you, pines, will rise
majestic into the skies.

The Amicable Stars

after Jorge Guillén, "A la vista"

Amidst the sonorous night the stars
accompany our minutes and hours
inaudibly to the human ear.

With a shrewd brilliance they glitter and
resolve: configured, atremble, above
the many mysteries. Never unsure.

We're tormented by our understanding?
Those huge spaces will always leave us
shy before their outrageous immensity.

Space beyond space ... of withheld revelation
so far apart from our thought, that it calls:
Wait; don't give yourselves up to delirium.

The sky over our hearths is housing –
familiar, and well-named – these stars, who,
paradoxically, become friends.

from *Against the Flight of Spring*
(2013)

Into Twilight

after Juan Ramón Jiménez, "Luz Ultima"

Late gleams, at play on the tips of the woodland crown –

quavering, you toss and scatter as though
the fallen sun cut you loose and has let you go.

Tumbled apart with the wind over dim branches,
what else is left for you now that the source is down?

Shimmer yourselves across to this blank leafage
hoisted against the encompassing grievous dark.

Transmute your gold through my pencil-slim near-reaches.

Together, let's leave a durable mark.

Grandparents

I never wondered aloud, nor was told in their house,
much about cranky Grampy – stooped, frail, thin, bald –
or, twice his girth, gentle Grammy, the plainest old woman
I'd seen, with her welcoming magnetic smile.

Dense-grey German accents with simplistic word-stores
left them quite childlike to me, and made quainter
the salt-thrower superstitions that strained my mom's patience;
though mostly they both drew a reverence I fully shared.

His wellworn carpentry tools rasped fragrant wood shavings.
He'd fix anything. She cooked roasts, mashed potatoes, peas, beets,
and thick-crusted pies. Beans and carrots were tended out back,
in front red roses. Indoors, velvet African violets. A lilac
stood at the side toward the engine plant's large parking lot.

*

Summers, he'd pluck the metal beetles off the roses,
drop them in oil. She laundered, crocheted and sewed.
Groucho would make him laugh. Sometimes I heard whispers
of his daily pass through Luther's Bible's block script.
Grammy prayed silently. Often just cleaned and scrubbed.

Twice Grampy rowed me around Broadbrook pond after sunfish
and pumpkinseed; spoke little, shared sweet butterscotch.
Mom later said he was palace guard to the Tsarina,
chosen for height; fled ahead of the Japanese war
to toil on the Panama Canal. Yellow fever. Then coalmine.

Disinherited too, she came for new life in New York.
Began as a maid to a generous rich Jewish lady.
Sang a lot when still young, mom recalled. "Lovely voice."
Raised four kids, worked in the plant when it made rugs.
In her bigflowered dress, Grammy always gave me the best hugs.

Child of Self

"I am my own child," the great poet said in his pride.
And what, and whose child, if any, ever, am I?

"I am my own man," I could say. "Unbeholden. The Chief."
(Maybe give myself a slight raise now, and extra time off!)

I was, am, the boy of my father, genetics affirms,
though more of my mother, in complex emotional terms.

In Dad's near-absence I struggled to clear my own slate:
in body, mind, heart, securing a private estate.

As if there were any choice in this entire matter.
As if some centre could cohere, not divide and not scatter.

Nor could I locate a mentor or real role model.
Gained a crude patience, muddling thru fast working-years.

Avoided much, withheld the thoughts that I made mine alone.
Or so it seemed. Observed, listened, got over small fears.

Waiting for what – a greengold gate to spring on its own?
Leaving the debt to the infant-within in arrears ...

Today I'm a father and double as both parents too,
with dwindling time for bridging old rifts before I go.

To pull that off, in full, I'd best solve my sole self first.
I carry this fraternal twin in me, past-due its birth.

The Partner

This life tears on, through progress and decay.
Past lives lie killed, while in the frantic present
one fades fast unless joltingly renascent.

It seems I'm frankensteined by innovation
that flattens futures into instants gone
and fouls the fields loved under antique dawn.

If not for *your* long constant new creation,
my spirit would be void of scope for play.
I'd lurch in shrouding whirlwinds of dismay.

You fortify a space to temper rages,
outmode regret, by timely consummation,
and charge me with a use for troubled age.

Compass

homage to Sonnet 116

I'll only smooth the path for the wise pair
who love each other wholly as they are
and as they will be: never in despair
at wounds of change, hostile desire, or fear.

Those ones have powers that, through droughts and floods,
guide them more soundly than a satellite
beams GPS across the longitudes.

Free radicals and the earth's weight will fright
the slack skin crinkling over bending bones,
while titled waves of days accelerate;

but stronger care won't bow to such unknowns.
It shines with courage and warm tolerance
despite what dizzy media dictate.

I learn this, making real my own romance.

Clarities

One night I saw my name written in cloud
but afterward kept questioning who I am.
My own script seemed like rows of aimless puffs
whose hollow thunder could portend no rain.

Some said, we need to trek into strange lands,
live lean, bear pain, and more than flirt with danger.
Converge on the adverse, clasp its hard hand.

Instead, seldom excursing from the nests
of harmless work and pleasure, I hung back
oblivious to the unknown deity
who speaks, at last, through terror of Her lack:

*Not knowledge nor experience; by faith find
the full and empty clarities that sign
the presence in the desert of our words.*

Trajectories

Lees of the sun do their nightly dissolve.
My little path, too, dries and dims.
    I'm scraping what's left aboveground,
    that could colour up dreams.

I starved this day's wish to out-glare
the pointblank of noon or at least upend
    the narrowing expectations
    in the eyes of my friends.

The cosmos roars on toward dispersal
in backdrop soup or sucking holes –
    while we ourselves have inflated
    the melee and sped the falls.

Still, though, on a quiet day I hear
surviving bees' earnest work
    to remake future roses: out
    from compost, against this quick dark.

Nowhere Here

"going where I have to go" – *Theodore Roethke*

I have to go off-world. This little one
is overrun with noise and fume and speed.
It's undermined by fear. The clever greed
that drives the mighty to trademark the sun,

to hoard its warmth. A universal stun,
if not pained lonely in addictive need;
bamboozled by the most simplistic creed.
Soft touches lost at every handhold won.

Off-world I go. Not giving up my being
in violent despair. Not on a tear
with some intoxicant. Not lamely fleeing

to rustic resort, retreat anywhere
ascetic or remote. The one flight freeing
from all such   is imagination's care.

Nocturne

For once, a calm wide open night
pierces with less-thin constellations,
like those before the rise of cities –
felt, not nostalgically, but by sheer
subsidence onto what was, and is.

In noiseless trance the grey veil withdraws
from nighthawk, below shooting star:
a cool salve spreads over broken slopes
and a breath blooms back among the names
of owl, and firefly, milky way

Against the Flight of Spring

Oak tree and locust tree, slow to leaf,
prolong the Spring by a common reserve,
admitting sunshine through still-bare limbs
on accents of fragrant phlox, white anemone:

all to the chorus of the tiny, fierce,
dainty warbler, the loud brazen jay,
pert-whistled cardinal, loquacious wren;
each proclaiming their open terrain,

only to subside in fast-mounted heat,
darting less often through slenderer gaps
with underleaf-pale or rich-colour flickerings,
like scattered recollections of forgetting;

while just a few keep their retrograde outcry
apart from the rush to be earth's.

The Spruce We Saw

near Port Renfrew, Vancouver Island

Evening was descending on the narrow road
that twisted with creeks under fir-covered slopes
and by breaks into stony, scrubby clearcuts.
The moss-hung boughs we passed along the banks
played half-familiar Island repetitions
of varying strangeness. Then on the local map
you saw the words "Giant Spruce," and so I
was set to stop when a small sign announced
"Harris Creek Spruce." A short path led in through
a grove of thinner trunks toward one dark girth.

It had begun to rain and you chose to stay
inside the car. You said only much later
you felt uncommon darkness radiating.
Not feeling any such thing, I approached.
A moss-streaked bole rose up, more broadly-spread
than any I had seen – multi-flared base
like that of an old Soviet rocket, massed
as necessary to uplift the long ascension
of the black pillar's dozen-foot vast width,
stretched almost undiminishing, on and on,
until lost in great darkgreen upper branches.

Reaching, I touched the bole's cool soft surface.
Just seconds after, somewhere overhead,
a single crack of thunder detonated.

Then I felt, more inference than feeling:
this is a being; nothing of our day
sticks to it. Pillar darker into *black*
than that word or its idea could relate.
This entity that claims its own dimensions,
in midnight of a nonhuman awareness.
This tall simplicity, aloof from sun,
from civil knowledge, without the least link
to heart or hand. Lone, in-itself shrining,
hermetic, in full alien plenitude.
Utterly other.

— Though later you surprised me with the claim
you sensed a "vortex" (and then I no longer doubted
it was well you'd kept away). "Nothing
malign," you said; slow swirl of primal power.

And once I'd safely driven off, you told me
that you had looked back: and saw, high-up,
two prongs, or horns, protruding from the crown.

Of the Painted North

at the McMichael Canadian Collection

In between back-here and out-there the great forms convene:
angling wide, shifting, held slow among strokes of cold colours.

Up from the gravid dark, their long-range, marshalled contours
press against *no more*, toward *this is* and at *we have been*.

Sky, waters, cloud, rock, trees, by stormy alliance
with human touches, resist the inconsequent past.
They sign beyond stillness, in deft-handed gestures made fast:

non-animate yet alive across listening silence.

Soulless, ensouled. Deep-aloft, implicate on-below:
as, throughout bleak fleet watercourses of dispersion,
ripple far whispers, ingrown motions, calmer immersions –

their tough artifices. Heart-stone, bedded in that flow.

The unsettleable lands rise, which we dream we can know.
Tumult smoothes, wrested asway through the blue fluent snow.

In a Room of Milnes

at the Art Gallery of Ontario

How cold these are. And still. A dim
patina shrouds each one. And, from
inside the surfaces, there leaks
a shadowiness. Old shadings.

Drab, almost. A certain dullness creeps
into the very colours, even orange,
even red. Muted, scratchy. Scrape-like. Thin.
And yet a subtle lunar glow

comes on. A rooftop slants palely away
and back; dark swaths of evergreens
bristle, recede. Blank lakewater,
and a snow-covered meadow, float,

a hill rises in air. Some clouds
cloud. And re-cloud. Then transparence
of a simple glass jar gives out
plain white gleams at the lip and neck.

Mere tilt of a pole, shape of a shed,
a staid plank-sided house or cabin – how
their posed suggestions co-irrupt
forsaken spaces into presences,

and bring on a full emptying of time.
Resistance to oblivion. Between motion
and stasis. How thoroughly each
patch of texture gains a careful warmth

and infra-human tone. – Not comforting,
but still a rough assurance. Open. Broached.
How they each, then, do move. Move into us.
To stay: insistent. Stay. And stay.

Fungi near Lost Lake

Down the path into the woods, through subsiding showers,
the band of friends makes its way toward Lost Lake.
Sunbreaks flashing between clouds, with liquid sparks,
enrich the red/gold leaves flamed overhead
and glistening underfoot … when we start seeing,

half-buried in leaf-fall, shelved and enclustered
toadstool, lush honey-leather, puff, comb-coral.
Cap, crust, ruff, button, cone, or garish dotted slime.
The transient genitalia of the undersoil,
whose non-mortal offspring thrive in unknown dark.

Those pale micelial threads, extruding and probing,
are not just rootlets, mouth-parts, gut-tracts alone.
Interlaced all-around, through indefinite wide yards,
their species possess and rule all the nether-woods.
Far more than conduits drunk with existence, they

are at-work intellects. Intent neural nets
spread useful data about. Multifarious
minders, tenacious laboratories, they test
the composition of bordering compost,
send scouts of themselves on open-ended quests.

They relegate relic forms into formlessness,
break toxins down, neutralizing their threat,
transform what's moribund into the stuff
of relentless vitality under the carpet
of death. Are symbiotes, too, with the upright trees.

We tramp aboveground in alien ignorance
of labyrinthine tubules aloof from our air,
remote from sense and thought's grasp almost utterly:
well-buried, much like the links back to our innards,
behind the lighthoused coastlines of our brains.

Their infra-spreads become the capillaries
for gross benevolence. As if – so it would seem –
their reality were centrally non-malefic.
As if the whole below-ness for which they are proxy
outmassed the sunned Manicheanism of things.

Could, then, one of our longest-unmet longings
be to re-root and re-merge in the dark of earth,
becoming threaded somehow through that substrate,
de-centred there, in amorphous bliss? What new fruit
might mount, for a good while, from the source below?

                    *

Now the companions emerge from half-shadow
onto the stone lip, to stare through lifting mist
at arrayed warm trees across a grey water's
undulant quavers and small intersecting waves.
Water: long-circular in-constant fundament …

Soon that sought lake, and the remembrance of seeking,
will leave a porous moist loam upon dispersion:
its melt of lonesomeness, of walls of the strange.
So it's not foliant light we will take with us,
off the nether of unspoken bond and mesh,

but a strong friendly embrace, tended onward,
through the broad networks from which each of us came –
outside the powers that pile plastic and steel;
in the rich soil of persistent affection,
living less for *what I want*, than by *how we feel.*

Songbird,

          the sky you bring down so near,
unst(r)ained by any weight or dull soil,
confers transparence of heart that draws
immediate soul from springs below
your piccolo throat
            without a claim
to dominion – but yet a dweller
beyond the clutches of desire,
when all the call-notes plash and pierce through.

We are flown free: a moment plum(b)ed, winged
in the ear of the one, only song.

free-flight

homage to José Acquelin

you hear the bird as you do, thanks to your star
in moments when logic itself seems mirage
breaking the habit of dust

and all at once mobility needs no wing
and in this universe off its edges
the dark in your light lifts like fog

Give praise

bird-like, unto the given
blue of resounding blue silence over

shimmery goldleaf-gold as it flies
atop a lone yellow maple – riven

through the whole time we are ripped alive
from image on into memory   driven

to sing the gain in the sound that plies
the waking wind-swirl after we sever

by dint of a less frangible ash,
which won't shake loose from the score of its cries

(marrowed and feathered with fire)
until the reverse of forever

from *River Neither*
(2015)

Aerial Ones

We fly – or is it fall – without fix,
heading our hearts through the ring of air
on earth's bell, swung around the sun's well
by motherly gravity, loving
to bob and dip while beaten and wrung
under those wind-shifted rafters, clouds,
at our unknown removes from the rim.

Your longing

          comes out of
absence from an Eden
displaced impossibly
to vague futurity.

It pulls toward a return
to brightness you never
knew aright: rainbow-bent,
glimpsed for a wild instant.

More than a homeland-space,
more than the fast embrace
of an only Other,
friendliest of lovers,

it's release from desire,
repair for sore losses,
enclosure, pole on pole,
and, at last, being whole.

So its bearings fasten
on states that cannot be,
ones that have never been,
unto eternity:

before birth, after death.

Still, it keeps us dreamers
leaning on, past the end
of torn heart, of split mind:
breathing a farther breath.

Animal Thoughts

They prowl with ease, as though it must suffice
to feed and breed and be, then go away.

No inkling of an immortality,
even in species. Each one has its day –
or many millions, down the stretching chain.

Dim origin, on toward a nighted close.
Behind, beyond – a void. Worth final pain?

Not near enough, *for us,* just to have been,
and left some genes for dim posterity.

The ways a person's acts will ramify,
diffusively, tell more than we suppose.

Best questionings do not beg fast replies.

The curious looks a cat shines at your eyes
mimic your inner scans for deities.

Late Poem to Mother

You told me a constant cloud shaded you overhead,
and, in that climate, determined upon "sacrifice,"
believing, as long as your children were wholesomely bred,
we'd draw down more sun, both achieve and be upright and wise.

With your aim to stretch me well-past what came easy and loose
you spun finer fabric than any threads I'd ever choose.
So what do I make of gold patches now strained through the blues?

Late Poem to Father

It would seem that a ghostly Victorian inhibition,
joined in some semi-archaic, male-only bind,
clamped cool retardant ahead of emotion's ignition.
Hunting and feasting – the primary joys you divined.

Whether there was any use in what seemed like neglect,
I'm glad you and I settled at last on cautious respect,
almost, for paths and wide views which would not intersect.

A Mythic Witness

for my father

I witness, not so much "for the Defense"
as for a counter-myth, and being aware.
My testimony speaks without pretence
of grasping truth or justice – but with care.

Disdaining my ineptitude seems fair.
The daydreams, the deficient common sense.

Exposure to deep woods in mountain air
transformed fear into awe at the immense.
I fumbled objects thrust toward unsure hands,
but long legs worked us far up the wild lands
outside soft pity, free from grid and clock.

If there were not bonds to you, there did grow bands
whose lonely sinew stretched me to take stock –
through you, of what made mud, of what was rock.

A Reclamation

for my mother

Is it the final cliff that we must measure,
or the warm valleys the slight peaks inform?
What was most fleeting can hold fuller treasure.
Even the lulls. And fresh wind, after storm.

So much of early childhood flowed with sweetness.
Left to imagine – learning the softest way –
buffered from scorn, from anxious incompleteness,
boding no chasm between labour and play.

Though that meant some steep interests would be paid
with thin reserves for fending fraud and force,
another stream ran on, whose banks weren't swayed
from its autonomous, initial course.

I draw upon and sail the river, still,
whose source you once vouchsafed. Through good. Through ill.

The Song

Wait, quiet, in a good place.
Birds will come.

The best song is loosed there
without intent.

Is its own purpose.
Let that too be yours.

Not court, and not impress
nor warn away.

Please merely, even when
listeners are one.

Out of the Woods

It's both the walking-through and the stilled presence.
They form their lively union, to create
the sense you are immersed amid the essence
of an entirely deeper, higher state.

Walled habit and the tides of time abate,
pierced and withstood at sudden coalescence
with these caresses through the windblown trees,
this clearance toward lake shore, on lichened rock:

in realization, here, how simplest ease
and quietude dislodge the chronic block

and let strong thought assuage while vision heals,
loosened from prior or proposed intent,
affirming all the breathing body feels
when it exists the way such things are meant.

Ask

Then who can sight the shadows on the wind,
or hear a single note sung by a stone?

Within a calm, feel how the evening light
sighs to diminish. Sense the pain of dawn.

Think the chaotic torment with which clouds
assemble, swell, disperse.
                              Call up the grief
in vanished language, in bulldozed belief.

Ask dying fish what difference: fire and mud.

Tread far enough apart from fear's refrain
to match the pace a forest would have strode
into a meadow, had it not been paved.

Ask through the unlit chambers down your brain.

Ask the last frog, last bird of a species
whether your fouling nest might yet be saved.

An Outdoor Vigil

Breathing is well. Half consciously, *breathe deeper*.
Draw an inch more of green scent down your lungs.
Maybe now see the tree-branches as rungs
on an ascent that isn't any steeper

for the mind's eye than to search tips of tongues
that name each darting bird, or the "spring peeper,"
or spot the resting place of that black leaper,
on a storm-broken bough.

               How you have clung
to safe, near shelves and even been a sleeper
in easy nightmare, not awakened song,
allowing as the norm what is plain wrong
with the exhausted air.
            You are a keeper
of slopes where the clear spirit still belongs.

Short Walk, Early June

The songbirds keep on calling through the rain
that soaks this warm green stillness, new in June.

Mild easy drops cannot unseat the ant
atop an orb of cloudburst peony-bloom.

A warbler cascades notes in twisty skeins.
Here on my knuckle lands the first mosquito.

Though locusts' frills are browning, the perfume
persists, and lilacs hold their purple tone.

… redolent of those once loved who are gone.
… opening further ways to feel alone.

Yet nothing here, or far, can dampen fully.
It seems a given gift, to feel at all.

Near pleasure seeps across this melancholy,
and thorns of loss mist over, past recall.

River Neither

A dusty cul-de-sac? A sky thinned into space?
We could regard our end as both, or either.

Instead, let us observe the River Neither.
Calmed by some dams (extracting power where falls
or rapids were) its whole vocation is,
unless men kill it, just to flow and be
flown its own sinuous way by gravity
and press of volume.
                      So it self-inscribes,
in gliding form along its shores of earth,
and lets frog and fish spawn and swim and leap,
the ducks dive, that rest now among the ripples,
and reeds, weeds and the willows drink their fill.

It also lets these eyes drink, swayed and smoothed
by the inevitable gracious motion, here
on this resplendent day, far-between flood and drought.

Along its other bank: a swan with cygnets,
passed by a young tour-boating party rapt
in progress of a quaint harmonic song;
near where tall yellow flowers mime the sun.

Such moments have sides but no source or mouth.
The ocean, where this goes but does not end,
is gatherer and widest of the rivers.

What else will write the script that can declare
we're neither earth nor fire, nor plain air?

Curled notes

above-ground, even in decay,
or still more briefly on the living air,
greet and infuse fleeting reality –
what some power outside time originates,
and what time's power in time obliterates,
taking all with it, soon, if not today.

For now, how brightly the sun's fragments flare
off blueblack wavelets; float, in diamond-sparks,
a moment clear, before each blinks back, dark.

How luminous and florid, dying, are
the stained leaves that strain through this windy shine.
Their rustle mixes an almost resigned
sigh with a fey denial, as if seeing
no use but the whole tone of their being.

Octobering

Away from what is not mine, out toward what
　　next blend of beauty, ripeness and decline ...?
Or might I front, down steeper paths of thought,
　　some earthly light that verges on divine.

What illustrates the panes of stained-glass leaves,
　　sparks through a chipmunk foraging black branches,
knocks in the woodpecker's hard beak that cleaves
　　dead bark? From a live limb, a robin launches ...

Each being feeds and flees in its one form.
　　The chill air rendered by the ordained sun
drives mass provision for the certain storm
　　which will rake every thing until it's gone.

My homing swerve must alter such a note:
make an embracing cry flash past this throat.

The Ice-stormed Trees

They outlive us, we thought. Parental, shading
our little statures. Forms admired, when noticed.
Even all bare, the sleepy Mandelbrots
of twigful leaf-shaped wholes gave soothing pleasure.

A light but steady rain on frozen boughs
soon candies them in gleaming crystalline coats.

Ice weighs, the cold wood bends, and then we hear
the sharp, shot-like report, brief crackle and tinklings.
And look: the shock of bare tan strip and spike
above, and a downed thick limb, in shattered sprawl.

Upward, the intact arrays bloom unreal sparkles
when power flicks on and later sun bejewels.

Now vision tips, past lacquering excesses,
into debris new leaden thoughts can't haul.

Supra-natural

Fine farewell glow, revert me to the dawn
of rapture at leaf-motion, on the fly,
tugging the heart afresh like that bird-wing
flashed from a bare branch in sun's orange eye.

There, too: the yellow-glistening poplar-tips
twirl more than naturally. Remind, how Nature
lights past herself wherever her glance grips,
and gives peep-holes – or swaths of revelation,

such as that pale-veiled westward cloud formation,
still to be coloured by the levelling sun,
angelic at far moveless distance, drawn
away from round mundanity's hoarse moan.

Steeped with these mortal eyes' imparting tone,
it shines, trans-human, while the earth spins on.

Sounded

at the Festival of the Sound

This blue dome suspends earthly gravity,
causing air's upward moisture to be made
to gather as a cloud. With levity
it sculpts itself in sunlight over shade,

gaining a character of deep elation
by almost imperceptible increase,
on vision rising toward a joint creation:
steadier than, yet fresh as, the lake-breeze.

Such lofty motion holds within the eye
much like a cascade will: white contour seeming
a fluid bridge from source to destiny
that, while it falls, keeps upright with a gleaming

carried beyond dim spume and passionate spray,
till even words for these things drift away.

*

Neither the score, then, nor a breathtaking
performance which entrances and transports
gives access to the threshold of their making.

The toneless tone, sounded the moment after,
answers the hush before the first note starts
the full dissolve along the fluent rapture.

So far-flown is it from the worldly riot
into the echoing concord of the parts,
that we unite with blissful fulfilled quiet
outside the bloodstream circling through our hearts,

until all hands cloud-burst their rough applause
(unanimous, unstinted gratitude)
for time held in embrace while brought to pause

at this convergence on beatitude.

Acceptance

It might have turned out altogether worse.
You never climbed by letting others down;
did not entrench your life in one dimension.

There's no shame when you've pitted good intention
against forces that stonewall, drain, or drown.
To feel "all wet" is both blessing and curse.

So what, if nothing you achieve gets mention
across the blogosphere. Reverse
of privacy is one gown you won't own.

Better to be a knower than be known.
Let others tout the trophy and the purse.

Alert along the margins of invention,
you incur little envy, less remorse.

Flight Home

The limbo of not being on the earth with you,
flung loose from time-zone and place, in a cylinder
seven miles up, is by no means dissimilar
to other separations, past and due.

I gaze at, but can't graze, the groundwork of things.
My moody imaginings too pinned to soar:
tin-wrapper'd, cased in the thin-airy roar
the metal and engine suspend on fixed wings.

Tended by attendants, anonymous rows
impassively couched, cramped and canned.
Stretching, I let blood revisit my toes.
Uncomforted, except by faith that knows

distance is finite ... shrunken ... has been spanned
by the light of your smile, the clasp of your hand.

I and You

I find myself questioning who I am, but never you.
   You move with ease along ineluctable tangents.

I'm most alive "as the crow flies" – on, toward somewhere new.
   You gather all that you seek in the nearby contingence.

I feel a steady expansiveness, a pull beyond.
   You note more value for things I deemed matter-of-fact.

I hide stray wishes to swim outside my social pond.
   You fuse forthright care and warmth with the most gracious tact.

I listen at dissonance which foreruns euphony.
   You're drawn by wholesome ideals but possess second sight.

I hear voices through a half-awakened reverie.
   You sometimes cry out at dreams down the depths of the night.

I give thanks for the length of slack you will allow.
   You surpass what I once, long ago, dreamt – here and now.

New Poems

A*O

The alpha scent – of new flower yet-unnamed.
   … A beauty fearsome also, in its way.

I too am flower, nodding in the wind –
   give back some light with fragrance on my words,
   let them fly off along the charging air,
   be heard or not, but be what I must make them –
as what was necessary through my stalk.

Why else did I break from omega's ground?

In the Healing Park

Across the fresh light wind, a slanting sunshine
brightens the trees and their luminous flowers.
They raise my spirit. I enter among them
to be as I am, inseparably
with verdant force in green identity.

All of this hour's creation is rounding.
Violets, in profuse beds, abounding.
White apple-blooms unload lucent fragrance.
Up a high willow-bough hangs a greygreen bag
of nest. The oriole busy inside it
prods a new curve through the thickening weave.

Over the grass go undulant flashes
of goldfinch. A pert cardinal keeps firing
his piercing one-colour song.
                              This compact region,
more stressed each year, flares vital resilience
despite many ash trees cut down, against borers,
others with roots undermined, limbs dead-dry.

On saplings in the cleared space, leaflets flutter.
Their sticky juice gives off delicious tangs.

Every sensation becomes a green spark.

One must do no less now than transport melody
homeward that will dispel dust and the dark.

Prior Allegiance

You see only the oncoming abundance; I, a loss.
Trees, plants that rise all prettily dressed – full-frilled –
no, I don't underplay their breadth and triumph;

merely lament that earth's hourglass will so soon touch
the perihelion of ultimate green, and then, as if
in consequence, dry withering tan comes next.

Affection for the earlier shoots and buds near bloom
cannot eclipse. Those parted friends may well (as you
could say) have run their spans through bounds assigned.

Still, I glimpse ghostly traces, at that partial completeness
across the screen back of the eye – the flickering-faced
penumbras which refuse to ever lie sealed off.

They'll keep, down every looming phase and mood I enter,
beyond the furious lush, unstable solstice: onward,
into my own short given spread of fall –
                                        and now
I come to wonder, won't you yourself, some lone day,
before rain, after storm or worse, turn, feeling likewise?
Then will the same allegiance win you, too?

Green Thought from Summer Shade

The words do not attach to things. – *Emerge*
is what they mean to do. Describe, alone,
and you will only skim, extract, abstract

and circumscribe. So the full green, in leaf,
comes as a rhythm, a vibration. Pulses.
Blooms in the eye through breathing air. Sounds out

its colour all-across its range of tones.
Green verdure, flickering up at sky, or stilled,
consistent with the whims of the drawn wind.

… How many tinted hues, out of the basal
chlorophyll. Recessive, into near-black shade,
and shining, promontoried, blanched in sunlight:

offering us images of vivid splendour
or a calm radiance, while back, behind,
inviting refuge, gloom and mystery

in an indefinite mix. From which, birdsong,
well interspersed with virtual dim silence
(but for the shush of gusted, sailing boughs)

breaks, or shimmers momentarily.
Along its edge then floats the ecstasy
of plain white butterflies, lone, and in pairs

that verge for a brief bout of aerial combat
or courtship-gesture – until, just an instant,
I am with one, in flight, before my words.

A Death-match

Near the sidewalk on Yonge Street, between
Thornhill golf courses, where the small hill
slopes up, seeing some milkweed I thought
of the threatened monarch – and, right then,
one landed on a sprig of pink flowers.
This gave a lift, as if my own hope
or fancy somehow brought it about.

Now through the air above brisk traffic,
two goldfinches, glowing like small suns,
collide and, pecking furiously,
crash in a ball on the asphalt, but
keep pecking, for a second, before
a car whooshes over them, spilling,
tumbling, breaking them there in the road.

Surely dead, when the next car made one
into yellow-white rag with red streak.

Had they fallen on grass, the combat
could well have reached the same end. I'd heard:
hummingbirds kill each other. These, too?

What "selection" was achieved? Maybe
survival of the meek. More likely,
a culling of surplus males. … Though stunned,
I also resented this assault
on reverie. My mood skewed. It seemed
unnatural if not inhuman.

Zealots fanatic for zero sum
and absolute victory will dare
mutual annihilation. There
were merely these two cancelled finches.

Communal Trees

after reading The Hidden Life of Trees by Peter Wohlleben

Having studied them for decades, a man writes
of how they share food through adjacent roots
according to the need of weaker ones
of the same kindred species. – And why not?

All trees fare better in community.
Close-knit, they signal each other by scent
as well as by their rootlets. Their proximity
will also shield the group from the stiffest winds.

They still have varying personalities
to go with different features. Variance, too,
gives health. Scope to adapt across the length
of centuries when even landscapes change.

They shelter their small offspring and nurture them.
The canopy of shade curbs the new growth,
maintaining it at a slow, measured rate:
seasoned for multi-hundred-year lifespans.

When they return to humus, that is one
more gift. It provides nourishment to all,
assisting the oncoming generation
in spaces cleared where saplings can grow tall.

And yes, there are further complexities –
mixed roles of fungi and of rival species,
aloft or under the carpet on the floor.
Insects and birds and beasts will help or harm.

Accidental and intended wounds.
Diseases, infestations to fight off –
with further efforts at cooperation,
for common, and seemingly greater, good.

Extravagant – or generous – flight of seeds:
millions, against the odds for one successor.
(Far better landing random among friends
than planted in monotonous, brief rows.)

Collaborative with the very air,
working a "fair trade" form of symbiosis.
Not altruists, merely benevolent.
No yen for disassociated gain.

They don't especially exist for us.
With an enlightened sense of world –
implicit forest, region, and whole globe –
they enjoy being. Mean to pass that on.

And might persist that way, if we could let them.

Ruin

You can imagine what is there
no longer, erect in mind's eye –
perhaps an arch, a roofline, tower –
only if you sometime saw
a comparable cathedral, mansion, stolid row
of workers' homes, intact, survivor of
artillery and bomb, of fire,
of earthquake, or of developers'
more lucrative demolitions.

What if, instead, all you can do
is gaze at the low remains with nothing more
to latch onto – extrapolate from – than
a few worn-down foundation stones,
a stub of column, maybe scrap of wall.
What qualities can they show, by
themselves, what value offer,
and what significance, if this
reduction is the total one can know?

What if what we, collectively,
are doing to the world that was –
its earlier human structures and
the natural realm they marred much less;
what if that process now leaves us, at most,
odd unrelated relics, ruined not just physically
but beyond comprehension? Only
(or not even) desolated memory?
A wipe of data, irrecoverable.

But is all lost? So much razed long ago
is digitized. Go google. Better, buy an app.
Download archival videos
and simulations. Take a virtual tour
of any edifice, outside and in. Reconstituted.
Still better, once new VR comes online,
immerse inside a holo, tailored, interactive
with your preferences. Some even
will offer something like the smell.

To Du Fu

712 -770

Such disparate worlds. But you call
far-across the abysses. From frail
hut after hut of right words, begun
in a once grand society bled
by insane ceaseless wars: worn down,
bowed as you were in ill health,
withdrawn beside the long waters
under desolate cirrus, wan moon
that, even so, gave, like an ablution,
your constellated lines: their fluent
image of being.
                 Poor and obscured,
seldom back home or for long at each refuge,
in threadbare cold, in sadness,
the fleeting reprieve with a friend,
the helpless compassion, bald grief, your cry
still issues its power to pierce
the dust laid down over ages
of collapsing kingdoms' ruins,
perennial guises of greed, wrath and pride,
the murk also of the clumsy translations –

to glass and distil and bring near
the most remote visions for those
who sip your moonlit wine as they rock
slowly there in the thin
but miraculous boat of the brain
that slips past blithe or brutish denial
and scorn of the historic warnings,
decline of mere solidarity
in a thoughtful existence. Of care. You,
who breathe improbable brotherhood
past every mask of despair.

Retirement Stance

Now my manoeuvring, my sideways tack
labours against the down-tilt of this tall
plateau – in gratitude that cliff or crack
seem far-removed. But it's not to protract
and preserve merely, not even with all
the goods I still hold (for which I again
give due thanks). It's mainly to link watercourses
and quarries with yet-unexhausted resources
one knows will be drawn upon, vein after vein:
persistent in reaches of mind, hand and heart
superfused by the mutual aid come from friend
unto friend – each of those who both stay and depart;
though that last group increases – along my lone bend.

Office Dream I

The cubicle with little desk where you
might still be called on to perform some remnants
of your old job's duties
has lost its walls. Fringed with dark foliage, it
lies open to the rain.

Office Dream II

New office tower, some hundred floors.
A former company, revamped, has hired you back.
You have a vague but high-level assignment.

Each day, their headquarters relocates
without your knowledge. At lunch hour
the eatery has moved. Nobody knows you.
Signage is missing or ambiguous.

You rehash the dull sense of insufficiency
from past years and a prior fear leaks back.
This world has morphed away beyond the grasp
of your old fading, obsolescent skill-set.

At a strange console for inputting codes
you strain to recall symbols long unused.

A sudden deadline looms for your lone project.
The specs they gave were not especially clear.
You arrive one day in your underwear.
Nobody notices.
                    It seems – so far –
you are the single person here who cares.

Morning Commute

We invent a perimeter of order.
We circle ourselves as best we can
with the readings and the estimates
that make some sense, even
of a strained ankle, scraped knee,
a fallen branch, a squirrel
flattened on the pavement.
These ordinary accidents that barely
graze us or distract a moment
from the momentum of complacency.

And then,
after the irritable endurance
of a traffic backup, see
the car, its front crushed on a tree,
a stretcher taken into the ambulance
with a covered shape.

This never could be us;
we drive defensively.
Our life continues blindly charmed.
There's no compassion called-for –
for the stranger. We skirt around.

One can't believe it never isn't "me."

Approach / avoidance

The neighbour in the rear-view mirror –
he's farther away than appears.

Persistent, though.

Let's keep it so. Our fears
for a collision yield safe separation
from single-lane *terroirs*.

A steady press toward the floor.
Sensing that the one behind
is too hopelessly other, altogether …

with a counter-hint of the bind
by which some are brothers who never
cross paths with me or you,

who elude as much as pursue.

In Flight

How thin the wings that lift us to our air
over the fleeting ground – that stiffly bear
the shakes of turbulence. Titanium,
bolted and cut into severest lightness,
at proven angles mastering such height.

Along our own plane, where we serve as pilot,
nobody mapped the final landing spot.

One solo charter. Hardly comprehending
our ported views, the clouds that streak their layer
to the horizon. Seeing how all we eye,
so large yet finite, races out of light.

And now we feel consumption's gauges quaver,
fuel and power drain, while wings fatigue.

What does it ever leave, beyond the contrail –
that speck, blinking against the gorge of night?

Dependence

There is a sense you could break totally down
under a swirling cone of stresses, dreads,
distorted panes. – That ill luck might well align
with subtle malice and sudden betrayal of roles
to drag you past the capacity to choose
resistance. Deflate all outward perspective; pour
blank darkness everywhere through paper-thin walls.

No way you can trust yourself now. Not alone.
You comprehend the need, far more than before,
to carry on in the ambit of others' care.
The hands that held you up and will wave you along
cannot at any time be only your own.

Our Path

We climb on through the wounds —
which are, after all, not fatal,
only mortal …
                        And so we will go,
whether safe or at risk, to earth,
to waters, toward skies of amenable stars
yet never be bound away
from true friends, in the long bond with them.

There is hurt. Even so I refuse
being sealed. I stride or limp after
what moves beyond all — which is also within
and gives lift to the load.
                        It undarks
at the knowing this path cannot shut:
how something far-in-us goes on,
reaches past the lone end.

Bridge

Here, hitting stride along the bridge of scars,
both prudence and necessity move me,
seldom gross danger now or chance embrace.

I called a truce in the circular wars
instigated to shiningly prove me
more than I am, or can be, at this pace.

I broke my last railing but still bend bars,
wary of each new abutment above me.
Muse on strange imagery streamed from deep space,

deflecting earth's rumour. Leave unsettled scores.
Love myself enough that others might love me –
till the whole span melts away, without trace.

The Slate

Unsure who you are, after all of this time ...

How much does it sap or hollow or rot
when you pose assurance that cloaks the old shame
at never attaining the height so long sought.

Mishap and circumstance can't share the blame.
You were given scope in each foray you fought,
every beachhead and oblique retreat.
                              Any claim
beyond a dead heat wants a far feat of thought –
although the debacles did limited harm
and you meant none.
                    – So what? It remains: the full weight
of benign intent must, itself, create the form
for your being. – Not so?
                         Go on, then. Clear the slate.
Shed your best gleam, ensoul the near homeworld in spite
of the prodigal day, the imminent night.

With More Modest Hope

What finer mode of service:
instead of dispelling illusion,
to labour to transmute
the menace at the base
by rhythmical soundings.

Weave them, so they relieve
a chafing, walled mind
from structure and stricture,
tell how the wound-in coil was never
the sole orderly force.

Roll back, or fend at least,
the ravenous borders.
Lamp their invasive dark and as well,
eclipse the glare
of unmerciful stars.

Suspend the tidal momentum
that scours toward core vaults. Then, let
careless or fervent words
no longer baffle and sting,
but sing through our sleep.

Afterword

Overview. All of the "Selected" poems in this book are from six collections published in 1998 to 2015. Most of the "New" poems appeared in my 2017 chapbook *Pod and Berry*. I chose to include 15-20 pages of poems in each of seven sections so as to give a balanced representation of the larger body of work. Each section could be read at one sitting. In making the selections I weighed multiple factors. The earliest two books were long out of print, and I believed this book could reach a larger audience than any of my previous books have done. An assemblage like this also offers readers who are already acquainted with my work a fresh way of encountering certain poems in changed settings.

Selection. I initially asked eight friends to list a few of their favourite poems from one or more of my books. Then I worked with poet and editor Elana Wolff to narrow down those choices and our own, and decide on the optimal order for each section. She and I sought to intersperse particularly strong poems that are largely unique with others that encapsulate major recurring themes. Readers of my previous books may be disappointed that places were not found for poems they especially like, but I believe the hard choices had the up side of enabling new and different dialogues.

Audience. While hoping to reach as many readers as possible, I think I have few illusions. The relatively small audience for books like this has been shrinking, and most of the readership is fellow poets. I stand in resistance to this trend, wanting my poems to be capable of being understood and enjoyed by non-poets. Thus I'm opposed, as well, to the notion that "difficult," narrowly specialized or esoteric poetry is necessarily supe-

rior to anything a general audience can appreciate. Which isn't
to say that patient effort may not be required on the reader's
part in order to deeply enjoy a poem and access the full value
it holds.

Musicality and Thought. From childhood on, the poetry I
liked appealed to me primarily through sound and rhythm, and
secondarily through the images it could conjure in my mind's
eye. I understood that poetry was, essentially, something else
besides a vehicle for explicit wisdom or source of information.
It could become meaningful enough without the need to deci-
pher or parse. As my education progressed, I did find it worth-
while to exert the intellectual effort to interpret classic poems
for the sake of a more thorough appreciation of the "what"
and the "how." But I don't think I was ever inclined to replace
the experience of a poem with an explanation, no matter how
insightful. Even so, I have come to realize that poetry can, in
the deepest sense, be a mode of thinking as well as of imagining
and of expressing strong emotions (all three together, in actual-
ity). Such thinking is of a different kind from any analytic, con-
ceptualizing activity in ordinary consciousness, and it eludes
transposition into such terms.

Foreground and Background. In any case, I want my poems to
be *enjoyed*, first and foremost, rather than studied. Heard, and
felt intuitively, not decoded or paraphrased. As I see it, the texts
can operate like musical scores which are performed through
reading. Sound, rhythm, and unfolding structure are founda-
tional and the sine qua non. Beyond this, I am aware that it
is helpful for readers if they know a little about the persons,
places, ideas and historical dimension behind the poems, indi-
vidually and collectively. After all, poems do not spring from a
vacuum but are (to some minimal degree, at least) grounded in,

and gain a certain measure of "character" from, specific loca-
tions and events in the poet's life and from readings of other
texts. The Notes that follow this Afterword provide particular
details meant to aid readers' understanding of background and
context. What follows here is intended to fill in a broader pic-
ture in other ways, while perhaps serving, as well, to limit a few
potential misunderstandings.

Pronouns. Poems are always open to being misconstrued. One
common error is the assumption that, when the pronoun "I"
is used, it designates the author in a narrowly literal sense. An
experience a poem describes is presumed to have happened to
the poet in exactly that way, when in truth the "I" is merely
a generic subjectivity into whose "shoes" the reader is being
induced to step. It is true that poems such as "Reedy River" and
"The Spruce We Saw" are based on actual incidents; and equally
true that the "I" of other poems (most obviously, those that are
versions of other poets' work, like "The Sprig" and "From the
Depths") is *not* their author. But this differentiation does not
ultimately matter a whole lot. If a poem is going about its busi-
ness as it should, and if the reader allows himself to be drawn
in, the "I" in it will effectively stand in for him, as much as for
anyone else. There are, in fact, gradations among, and within,
all of my poems between autobiographical testimony and com-
plete fiction.

Adaptations. One somewhat unusual component of this book is
also, I'm afraid, liable to be misjudged. Two dozen poems in the
first five sections are based closely enough on other poets' poems
that I have acknowledged the debt either below their titles or in
the Notes. While it is not uncommon to write poems "after" those
of other poets, the proportion of such poems and the variety of
approaches I have taken is definitely off the beaten track. There
are admirable precedents in the versions or "imitations" by Ezra

Pound and Robert Lowell of texts they could only get near through translations. Both were keenly interested not just in extending their own imaginative and artistic reach but in showing their readers poetic landscapes that had been unavailable in English. In some respects, I followed their lead, albeit on a less ambitious scale, and mostly taking greater liberties than they did with their sources. A few of my "adaptations" (as I like to call them) come close to being translations, but even they diverge from the originals – for what I regard as valid artistic reasons. Every such poem pays homage to the one it is modelled on: with the aim of a certain equivalence, not to mimic or echo. The original voice (to the extent I can imagine I hear it) was hybridized with my own voice or voices, while both the style and content spurred me to leave more familiar poetic zones for newer terrain. What better way to learn and grow in the art? I also share the Poundian or Lowellian desire for my readers to discover poets whose work they might well find as exciting as I do.

Chronology. The exact chronological order of my poems, whether in terms of when each was composed or their publication history, is too complex to sort out here. Although some evolution in subject, style and mood could conceivably be observed from *Weighted Light* on through to my "New" section, there is no clear linear progression, so far as I can tell. For one thing, I came to realize that all of the poems from the 1980s I thought were worth keeping needed further revision. Taking them and other poems to workshops and reading them in public in the later 80s and early 90s proved invaluable in testing out what was working more or less well. As is indicated in the Notes, I eventually rewrote certain ones, and simply held back others and only made small refinements, after as many as ten years. The maximum turnaround time eventually shortened, but I continue to reserve the right to keep tinkering even with published poems.

Influences. Apart from listening to music, the most thoroughly formative influence on my poetry was the classic literature I read in my student years. At first I was drawn especially to 19th and early 20th century poets. Later the range expanded to contemporary poetry and world literature in translation, and the expansion continues. American poets born in the first few decades of the 20th century had considerable appeal when I was beginning to try my hand at poetry more seriously – something that only proved possible after I transitioned from academia into steady office jobs in the I.T. field. Instead of listing all the Canadian and international poets whose work I have read closely and with intense enjoyment and admiration (since that list would be very long), I would just point out that those named in my Notes are not in all cases the ones from whom I have learned the most, or the only ones whose work I have held in the highest esteem. It was also inspiring, in the 80s and 90s, to hear and actually meet some of the most renowned poets of the time, such as Seamus Heaney and Derek Walcott, when they came to Toronto. They further impressed on me the value of hearing others' poetry and of reading one's own aloud.

Subject Matter. Although the poems in this book encompass all of the main recurring themes in my body of work, they do not fully represent every subject I have been preoccupied with literarily or otherwise. There is a slightly larger proportion of "nature"-themed poems in most of my books, and several rather gloomy poems in *Confluences* express my ecological anxieties more pointedly than any here. Also somewhat under-represented are poems exploring cosmological themes and on electronic technology. But I believe a few examples can effectively be representative of the rest. Poetry is such a versatile medium that no subject lies beyond its reach, and I constantly read poems on a broad range of topics besides those that are evident in my own work thus far. I believe that the endeavour to write well, however limited one's scope may seem (whether by "privileged" or accidental circumstance), is the paramount consideration. And, too, seemingly absent themes could still be implicit.

Two Cultures. Besides jazz and classical music, two of the life-long interests that are reflected in every one of my books are science (i.e., a scientifically-informed view of the world) and visual art (mostly individual works). I have never found the aesthetic and the scientific to be incompatible or of unequal importance. Ideas and vocabulary from science have informed and enriched my writing, even though I can't claim much more than a layman's grasp. Many encounters with painting and sculpture throughout my life have given me incalculable spirit-nourishment. The few poems on art in this book are indicative of that, and, as with my science-based poems, are only a portion of my writings on the subject.

Form. Some readers will notice a shift from the mostly "open" forms of the poems in my first two books to predominantly strict and traditional ones from *Interstellar* on. I suppose that forms and formal principles like sonnets and syllabics became increasingly seductive to the part of me that loves games and challenges along with architecture and musical structure. But then it could be noted that a sizeable number of my earlier poems also have stanzas and/or metre. The Author's Note in *River Neither* states that "Form in poetry is, for me, as much an end in itself as it is a means of conveying and representing anything besides itself (i.e., 'content'). The shape or pattern – rhythmical, musical, architectural – which poetic form lends to verbalized thoughts can, and should, I believe, produce aesthetic pleasure seemingly for its own sake, in the ways that art and music do. But in poetry, what then takes on at least equal importance is form's capacity, when it is suitably harnessed, to deliver insights about ourselves and the human situation *which would not otherwise be gained.* Far from being a mere container that imposes limits, form can actually serve to liberate and open up paths to new discoveries of all kinds." Notwithstanding that, my "New" poems happen to either be less formal than their recent predecessors or else take on different forms from those used before. Never a "formalist" exclusively, I have often bent or changed the prevailing rules.

Philosophy. Readers and reviewers have commented that many of my poems raise philosophical issues. I hope it will be understood that the attitudes and stances presented are speculative and that there is nothing systematic afoot. The poems are accepting of contradictions. They tolerate inconsistency. The paradoxical aspects of existence appeal to them. Their philosophizing, such as it is, tends to be situational and pluralist. That they also, by and large, imply certain common values and cleave to a few basic principles, presumed (or, at least desired) to be shared by their readers, will be fairly apparent. As for spiritual dimensions, I mainly want readers to sense their presence between the lines.

Commerce and Community. One advantage poetry gains in not being a viable means of income is that it will hardly ever be co-opted by the entertainment industry or turned into a commercial product. These days the academic world does facilitate a possible career in poetry, and I know, too, that there is modest financial support available through Arts Council grants, residencies at Libraries, independent courses and retreats, freelance editing, and so on. Much of the practical help poets get is on a volunteer basis, however. I have a lot of respect for those who manage, through talent and resourcefulness, to attain a kind of professional stature in the current climate. I am oriented more toward the grass roots and making connections with fellow writers who, whether young or advanced in years, are in the earlier stages of the development of their art. Others whose arcs I find appealing are those who manage to retain something of the proverbial "beginner's mind." I am also fortunate to have among my friends and acquaintances some of the finest poets in Canada. Collectively speaking, poets come in all shapes and sizes, with widely varying degrees of accomplishment. Each one's journey is unique, even if recurring patterns can be mapped. On my own journey I mostly steered clear of what I ambivalently regard as the institutionalization of poetry, while still aiming to be friendly and open to the entire range of poetic practice. Aware of divisions and discord but seeking to harmonize and unite and include. I have found that poetic art invariably benefits from the encouragement and constructive criticism its practitioners give each other both one-on-one and in groups. A geometric image stays with me, not of a pyramid on which competitive persons climb toward the top at others' expense, but of a *sphere* where value circulates and builds through mutually beneficial exchanges. Thus I always like to acknowledge and thank everybody who made a difference for me in this regard, helping create the sense I've gained of belonging in a diverse, ever-changing but always vibrant and supportive community. There is, as well, the immeasurable and continuing sustenance through the long bond with those who are no longer physically present. None of my books could have come about otherwise.

Notes

Poems from *Weighted Light*

"Mother and Girl" is based on two figures I saw from the Vaughan Road bus at the intersection with St. Clair Avenue in Toronto.

"Reedy River" reflects on an outing on a river in Algonquin Park. My maternal grandparents lived in Broad Brook, Connecticut.

"Golden Delicious" recalls a visit to Chudleigh's apple farm in Halton Hills, ON. The experiences behind, and the initial versions of, this poem and the previous two were all in the mid 1980s.

"In Curved Light" was triggered by the poem "Absence" by Jan Zwicky, in *Songs for Relinquishing the Earth* (1996). The setting is on the Bruce Peninsula.

"Waking" and the other poems by Paz which became the basis for poems in this book are in the bilingual volume *The Collected Poems of Octavio Paz 1957-1987* (New Directions, 1991). They were translated by Eliot Weinberger.

"The Sprig" emulates the translation of "La Piel del Abedul" by William O'Daly in *Winter Garden* (1986). This and several other poems emerged out of a study group led by Allen Sutterfield in the mid 90s, in which participants were encouraged to write "parallel" texts by following the sentence structure of the original while changing virtually all of the words.

"Antipodean" is a more free-wheeling emulation of Neruda's "The Lost Ones of the Forest," in the same book.

"Joe Henderson Quartet" celebrates a performance by the great tenor saxophone player and three excellent local musicians in Toronto in 1989.

"Fire Music" came in response to a phenomenal free-jazz performance in Toronto in 1997 by tenor saxophonist Charles Gayle, who also played piano and trumpet. For a time, Gayle had survived by busking on New York City street corners. According to theory, there was an infinitesimal bit of time in the Big Bang before all the laws of physics came into existence. Wild and "free" as this music sounds, it is not random or undisciplined.

Poems from *Unleaving*

"Leaf for Claire" is the oldest poem in any of my books. The first version, from 1982, was rewritten twice before publication in the zine *POEM* ten years later.

"In Farther Transit" owes a distant debt to a poem by Cavafy. It is from a period in the 90s when I regularly rode the Toronto subway and a bus to work.

"From the Depths" follows the German text quite closely, except that I Canadianized some of the images.

"Skin of Our Vision" drew on two short poems by Paz: "With Eyes Closed" and "Touch."

With "Venusian," I changed all of the metaphors while largely keeping the structure of Paz's poem in Weinberger's translation.

"Nerudaland" alludes to poems in several volumes by Neruda, especially *Residence on Earth, Canto General,* and *Fully Empowered (Plenos Poderes).*

"You artists" was inspired by Robinson Jeffers' "To the Stone-cutters."

"Sax" and "With Bass" and "And on Drums" stem from a sublime performance in the Toronto Downtown Jazz Festival in 1994 by Joe Henderson, Dave Holland and Al Foster. The three poems were first published together under the heading "The Trio" in the chapbook *The Tunnel Through the Trees* in 1999. One of the kinds of jazz I like best plays a whole lot of notes fast; and accordingly, each of these poems – if the reader can get up to speed with it – is meant to be read at a rapid clip.

Poems from *Interstellar*

"Solstice from an Office Tower" was originally titled "Solstice/ Top Floor." I wrote the initial draft when I had gone on a Saturday to my workplace on the then nearly deserted 20th floor of a building at Bay and Bloor Streets in Toronto. That version, from 1985, was completely recast in quatrains some fifteen years later.

"Pomona Solstice" is set in Pomona Mills Park, near my home in Thornhill, ON, as is "Solarities."

"Fossil Moth" came out of a weekend retreat near Collingwood, ON in 1992. The first version, written soon afterward, was extensively revised years later. It is one of several poems that recall the time when, age 10 to 12, I lived on Kodiak Island in southern Alaska. The surrounding mountains and shores became like an earthly paradise, soon to be lost.

"November Trees" was originally two separate poems, "Early November, Even Now" and "Two Weeks Later," which were printed on the same page of *Interstellar*. It is the first of many poems written in Pomona Park after I moved to Thornhill in 2003.

"Winter Night, Looking North" was paired, on facing pages, with a summer poem which also emulates one of Lampman's. I look on his poetry as belonging to a tradition, going back at least as far as Wordsworth and Keats, in which some of my poetry seeks, however distantly, to participate.

"Solarities" is the first of 17 poems on astronomical themes which made up the fourth and longest section of *Interstellar*. Most of these poems first appeared in the large-format art and poetry chapbook *Galactic Music* (2005). This book only includes the three least scientifically specialized of that series, which reflected on discoveries made by both probe (Voyager, Galileo, Cassini) and space telescope in recent decades.

"Interplanetary" alludes to "Spirit," the name of one of the two Mars rovers that landed in 2004, and to a line from Robert Frost's "Birches."

"Interstellar" quotes a phrase from the short poem "Brother-hood" by Paz, which has the subtitle "Homage to Claudius Pto-lemy." The "dour bard" is Ted Hughes. I would define "Hard SF" as speculative fiction that is primarily science-based.

Poems from *Confluences*

The first seven poems in this section first appeared in the large-format art and poetry chapbook *Temple of Fire* (2008), all of which is concerned with aspects of "antiquity" represented principally by ancient Greece. Some of these poems drew inspi-ration from the pen-and-ink drawings by my wife Holly which were reproduced in that book.

"If by War" was previously titled "At Heraclitean War."

"Hestia Exposed" is my one and only mythological poem.

"Autumn came" is the opening poem in the chapbook *The Tun-nel Through the Trees*. Revised for *Confluences*, it originated as a response to yet another of Neruda's *Winter Garden* poems.

"Call" was the result of a writing exercise given out by Michael Fraser, based on a passage in Paz's long poem "Sunstone."

At the time I wrote "Riddle" I was much taken with the para-doxical "Vertical Poetry" of Argentinian Roberto Juarroz.

"Two Kinds of Blues" came from an on-the-spot "themed poetry challenge" issued by James Dewar on one of the nights of his "Hot-Sauced Words" reading series.

"On Music" stays relatively close to the original German text, but I also consulted several translations, including Stephen Mitchell's.

"Du Fu's Pines" is a version of "The Four Pines" as translated by Rewi Alley in *Du Fu Selected Poems*, published in China by Foreign Languages Press.

"The Amicable Stars" was a response to Guillén's poem as translated by Cola Franzen in the bilingual *Horses in the Air and Other Poems*.

Poems from Against the *Flight of Spring*

The "Grandparents" are my maternal grandparents. My grandfather came from a German-speaking part of Lithuania which was under Russian rule. "Groucho" refers to Groucho Marx, when he hosted the TV quiz show *You Bet Your Life*.

"Child of Self" is one of ten poems I wrote on a two-week writers' retreat near Santiago, Chile led by Barry Dempster. The "great poet" is Neruda.

"Compass" answered a challenge made at a party given by Marja Moens, to write a version of Shakespeare's Sonnet CXVI using contemporary diction.

"Nowhere Here" came fully-formed out of another of James Dewar's "themed poetry challenges."

"Nocturne" and "free-flight" are two of a half-dozen poems I wrote in admiring response to the collection *The Man Who*

Delivers Clouds by Québec poet José Aquelin, translated by Antonio D'Alfonso (Guernica Editions, 2011).

"The Spruce We Saw" is the only poem in this book set specifically in a place outside Southern Ontario. It recounts an experience I and my wife had in 2010.

"In a Room of Milnes" was composed on-site in one of the rooms at the A.G.O. that displays landscape and still life paintings by David Milne.

"Fungi Near Lost Lake" came in the wake of one of the annual retreats I went on with friends in a wooded area east of Bracebridge, ON. I had recently read one of the scientific articles that were starting to appear about the vital role of fungi in forest ecosystems.

"Give praise" was inspired by a poem by Jiménez whose title is translated as "How the Bird Singing."

Poems from *River Neither*

"Late Poem to Mother" and "Late Poem to Father" began as separate 14-line sonnets in the LyricalMyrical chapbook *Twenty-eight Sonnets*. For *River Neither* I decided to reduce each one into a 7-line poem and place them on the same page.

"Out of the Woods" and "Curled notes" are among several short poems I composed in the vicinity of Lost Lake on retreats in 2013 and 2014.

"Outdoor Vigil" and "Supra-natural" were both composed in Pomona Mills Park.

"River Neither" has imagery from a late-summer visit to Stratford, ON.

"The Ice-stormed Trees" testifies to the damage from the storm that afflicted most of the Greater Toronto Area in 2014.

"Sounded" was begun shortly before and completed soon after a wonderful chamber concert at the annual Festival of the Sound in Parry Sound, ON.

"I and You" originated in a writing exercise given out by Sue Reynolds the only time I managed to attend her Inkslingers group at The Black Swan Tavern in Toronto.

New Poems

"In the Healing Park" and "Green Thought from Summer Shade" are yet again from Pomona Park.

The "Office Dream" diptych originated in a workshop led by Kim Aubrey at a writers' retreat in Bermuda in 2017. The participants were encouraged to write about their dreams. "A*O" was also written there.

"Communal Trees," like the "Fungi" poem in *Against the Flight of Spring*, is an unusual instance of what I consider to be yet another of the many "uses" of poetic art: to convey factual knowledge along with a form of moral instruction that neither lectures nor scolds.

First drafts of "Ruin" and "Morning Commute" were written in Kate Marshall Flaherty's StillPoint Writing Circles in 2018.

"To Du Fu" is in tribute to the classic Chinese poet whose work has resonated more powerfully with me than that of any other, even through stilted translations. Happily, there are multiple versions, and notes, available in English. Although he thought his work would be forgotten, Du Fu became possibly the most beloved of his country's poets even now.

"Our Path" is in memory of my friend James LaTrobe.

Acknowledgements

Some of the poems in this book appeared previously in the following journals, zines, and online publications: *The Ambassador, Hammered Out, Juniper, Lichen, POEM, p o e t r y z'o w n, Tower Poetry, Upstreet* (USA), *and Verse Afire* (The Ontario Poetry Society). Others were in the anthologies *Arborealis, Decebration, Delicate Impact, The Edges of Time* (Seraphim Editions, 1999), *Frost and Foliage, Heartwood* (League of Canadian Poets), *Latchkey Lyricality, Mix Six* (Mekler & Deahl, 1996), *Opus III: A Conspiracy in XV Variations, Poets for Life, Mindshadows, Renaissance Conspiracy, Renaissance Reloaded, Ropedancer,* the *Seeds* series from Hidden Brook Press, *Spirit Eyes and Fireflies, Tamaracks* (USA), *Transitory Tango, Understatement* (Seraphim Editions, 1996), *Windfall,* and *Winter Solitudes.*

I am particularly grateful to Elana Wolff for invaluable advice in selecting the poems, and to Ken Klonsky, Pierre L'Abbé, Donna Langevin, Al Moritz, John Reibetanz, Wendy Steginsky, and Russell Thornton for their helpful suggestions.

Reflecting on this book's long lead-up time, I'm filled with gratitude to all those who have encouraged and supported my writing and related endeavours, and opened doors for me year after year. That includes fellow poets in the following writing groups, starting in the mid 1980s: Phoenix, Allen Sutterfield's "Winter Garden" group, the "Paz Group," Donna Langevin's Art Bar group, the Expressionist Group, the watershedBooks poetry publishing co-op, the Vic Poets, Diane Mascherin and the Toronto Renaissance Conspiracy, the Vaughan Poets' Circle, Bunny Iskov's T.O.P.S. group, the Literary Lobsters, and Kate Marshall Flaherty's Still-Point Writing Circles. Deep appreciation and gratitude also go to Maureen Whyte of Seraphim Editions, Tai Grove of Hidden

Brook Press, David Zieroth of Alfred Gustav Press, Luciano Iaco-belli of LyricalMyrical Press, and my former partners and the staff at Quattro Books.

Beyond that, I feel extraordinarily fortunate to have participat-ed in the literary "community of communities" in the Toronto area and across Canada, and to have benefited so much from the prevailing goodwill and creative ferment that has continued to enliven our Scene with innumerable readings, launches, salons, and multimedia events ever since my first tentative forays into it four decades ago.

Special thanks to Michael Mirolla for his openness to a book of these dimensions, along with admiration for the extent to which Guernica Editions nurtures literary diversity in this country.

About the Author

Allan Briesmaster has been active on the Toronto-area literary scene since the 1980s. He began with Phoenix Poetry Workshop in 1985-1990. Later he became a reading series organizer (Art Bar Poetry Series and Toronto WordStage) and an events coordinator and volunteer. He was gradually able, outside of a series of day jobs in the IT field, to phase into editing and publishing work which became full-time in 2005. He was a member of the watershedBooks poetry-publishing co-op in 1997-2001, an editor for Seraphim Editions in 2000-2008, and a partner and editor in Quattro Books in 2006-2017. Since 2003 he has published limited-edition art and poetry chapbooks and full-length books with his own small press, Aeolus House.

Allan is the author of seven full-length books of poetry and nine shorter books. He has read his poetry, given talks, and hosted readings and book launches at venues from Victoria to St. John's. In 2017 he was awarded Life Membership in The League of Canadian Poets. He lives in Thornhill, Ontario (just north of Toronto) with his wife Holly, a visual artist whose drawings, collages and paintings have been reproduced in a number of his books and on some of their covers.